Spent

Spent

*Break the Buying Obsession and
Discover Your True Worth*

Sally Palaian, Ph.D.

HAZELDEN®

Hazelden
Center City, Minnesota 55012
hazelden.org

Library of Congress Cataloging-in-Publication Data
Palaian, Sally, 1958-
    Spent : break the buying obsession and discover your true worth / Sally Palaian.
        p. cm.
Includes bibliographical references.

ISBN 978-1-59285-699-2 (softcover)

1. Compulsive shopping. 2. Shopping—Psychological aspects. I. Title.
RC569.5.S56P35 2009
616.85'84—dc22

                        2009002470

Editor's note

Most of the stories in this book are based on actual events. The names and details may have been changed to protect the privacy of those mentioned in this publication. In some cases, composites have been created.

   This publication is not intended as a substitute for the advice of health care professionals. It is not meant to substitute for the advice of accountants, financial planners, or lawyers.

   Alcoholics Anonymous and AA are registered trademarks of Alcoholics Anonymous World Services, Inc.

        13   12   11   10   09   1   2   3   4   5   6

                Cover design by Theresa Gedig
        Interior design and typesetting by Kinne Design

*For my parents, who taught me that even though
money comes and money goes,
love, laughter, and family last forever.*

❖ Contents ❖

Author's Note xi

Acknowledgments xiii

PART 1

Money: A Complicated Problem

1. A Prevalent Problem 1
A Cultural Problem, 3
How This Book Will Help, 6

2. The Slippery Slope from Money Problems to Money Addiction 9
Criteria for Addictions, 12
Deprivation Money Addiction, 19
A Continuum of Money Behaviors, 20
When Money Addiction Overlaps with Other Conditions, 26
Summary, 29

3. The Emotional Sources of Money Problems 31
How Family Influences Money Behaviors, 32
How Outer Factors Influence Money Addiction, 39
Summary, 41

4. Types of Money Problems 43
The Materialism Continuum, 44
The Finance Continuum, 45
The Money Problems Matrix, 45
Indulgers, 47
Deprivers, 54
Combinations of Behaviors, 58
Summary, 58

5. How Money Problems Affect Relationships 61

Money in Relationships: The Inevitable Struggle, 63

Problem Users and Their Partners, 64

How Types of Money Problems Affect a Relationship, 66

When Partners Are Codependents, 68

When Two Problem Users Are Involved, 70

Problem Users Involved with Healthy Money Managers, 73

Summary, 74

PART 2

Solutions: Untangling Yourself

6. Your Personal Money Behaviors 77

Your Current Financial Behaviors, 77

Understanding Your Money History, 83

Summary, 88

7. Beginning Recovery 89

Six Phases of Recovery, 90

Phase 1: Hitting Bottom, 93

Phase 2: Accepting and Following Guidance, 97

Summary, 109

8. Life Visions and Spending Plans 111

Phase 3: Creating a Life Vision, 111

Phase 4: Living with a Spending Plan, 118

Learning to Make Healthy Spending Choices, 142

Banking Guidelines, 143

Summary, 146

**9. Phase 5: Changing Your Thinking, Feelings, and
Impulsive Actions** 147

Triggers, 147

Preventing Impulsive Spending, 159

Identifying and Coping with Relapse, 163

Summary, 168

10. Phase 6: Living the Abundant Life 169

Signs of Financial Health, 169

The Sense of Abundance, 171

Finding Balance, 171

Flexibility and Trust, 173

Emotional Authenticity, 174

A Unique Lifestyle, 174

Relationships, 176

Finding True Abundance Within, 177

Appendixes

Appendix A: Are You Codependent? 181

Appendix B: The Signs of Compulsive Debting 185

Appendix C: Forms and Blank Worksheets 187

Appendix D: Resources 213

Notes 217

About the Author 219

❖ Author's Note ❖

As this book goes to press, the world is in economic turmoil. Banks have changed their lending practices and credit has become more difficult to obtain for both individuals and businesses. Economists are forecasting that things may not improve for an indefinite period of time. Now, as a society, our challenge is to learn about our relationship with money so we can find the balance between financial survival and personal fulfillment. That's the message of this book, and it will be as timely in a prosperous economy as it is today.

In good times or bad, money issues can wreak havoc in our lives. My hope is that readers of this book will use it to begin a journey of self-discovery about the meaning of money in their lives. For those willing to embark on this uncommon path, there is hope and serenity.

. . .

❖ Acknowledgments ❖

Writing this book has taught me that hope and goodness lurk behind every mysterious corner. Wherever I turn, there are always generous and loving people. I would like to thank the following people.

First, my friends Eleanor Payson and Nancy Sparrow, for challenging me to teach and write about money dynamics; without them, I would be happily minding my own business.

Eleanor Payson and Linda Moody, for their unceasing support throughout the writing of this book and for gently nudging me to push through my avoidant and evasive antics.

Betsy Breckels Fortuna, for unconditional friendship and constructive feedback on this manuscript, and Clem Fortuna, for singing "The Impossible Dream" to us when we climbed out of the Grand Canyon.

Joe Kort, for humor, love, and writerly inspiration.

My very caring and generous siblings—Eve and Gary Ezmerlian, Carol and Steve Palaian, Terry and Chuck Palaian, and Laurie and Keith Neher. A special thanks to Lud for joyful playfulness always, and to Helen Kalayjian for tenderhearted, gentle support of my every endeavor.

My mentors Diane Blau, Barb Shumard, and Joy Messick, for seeing me, loving me, and encouraging my adventures. Thanks also to my colleagues and friends who helped me to live and develop the ideas in this book: Dave Balekdjian, Eileen Freedland, Connie Haley, Jane Libby, Jacqueline Polefka, Paul Duskey, Rena Seltzer, Joi Sherman, and Harry Taylor.

Ashlee Roberson, for her efficiency and ability to decipher my handwriting. Jeanne Ballew and Maureen Buchanan Jones, who helped shape early phases of this manuscript.

Thanks to Pat Schneider: lover of spunk, nurturer of souls, and cultivator of writers. Thanks to Cindy Barrilleaux, wordsmith and believer in this book, for not letting me collapse all those times I was exasperated.

Thanks to the staff at Hazelden—solid, good people who do important work.

Thanks to Vince Hyman, genius editor, miracle worker par excellence, kind soul, for asking important questions and working so darn hard to shape this book.

Thanks to my clients, who inspire me with hope and courage.

And to my partner, Gary Haelewyn, for bringing me childlike wonder and adventure, and for teaching me that love is the only treasure worth seeking.

. . .

PART
1

Money:
A Complicated Problem

A Prevalent Problem

Eric had already moved out of the house when he arrived at my office with his wife, Susan. He was quiet at first, seething with anger. When he spoke, his first words to Susan were loud ones: "I don't care why you do it. I can't take it anymore."

Unable to raise her head, and twirling a tissue between her fingers, she replied, "I know it's my fault. I don't even know why I do it." He had dragged her to therapy because he was tired of her dramatic excuses, and he was done paying for her spending habit.

Eric had bailed Susan out of debt three times over the course of their twenty-four-year marriage. This time it was for $67,000, the most ever. He found out by accident when her sister mentioned the credit card bill. Susan had been using her sister's address to receive credit card statements. Tired of the lies, and unsure about where he would get the money, Eric was furious.

Susan was trapped: she had to either get help to stop spending or lose her marriage. She had spent years staving off this dreaded day.

Susan began attending therapy to try to understand why she was so troubled. In therapy, she looked at her lifelong pattern and realized that she had always wanted to fit in. In third grade, she used her allowance to buy candy for her friends. As a teenager, she wore her mother's jewelry to school so she could impress her classmates. When her grandparents gave her birthday money, she spent it immediately on makeup or clothes for herself or gifts for her friends.

She recalled that her parents frequently argued about money. Her father was strict with money and often reminded the family of what he provided.

Even though her mother was practical about money, she was unable to convince her father to loosen up. Susan bypassed these fights by working at a bakery to pay for her own stylish clothes.

In college, she discovered credit cards. A local bank had set up a booth in the student lounge. She decided to apply. With credit cards, she was finally free from her father. She could buy what she wanted. In the first summer of college, she went to a rock concert in another state with her friends. She charged her meals and the gas when it was her turn to pay. She figured it wasn't a big deal; she could pay the minimum on the credit card, and she'd catch up during the school year when her dad was giving her money again. By the time she graduated, she had accumulated $9,000 on two credit cards. She thought it would be easy to pay off once she was employed professionally.

In therapy, Eric reminded Susan that she had never been totally truthful with him about her problems with money. When he looked back, he remembered that something wasn't right early on. Susan blew up and refused to talk about money during premarital counseling with the priest. Eventually, the priest's presence wore on her conscience, and she decided to tell Eric about her debt. She confessed to $8,000 on her credit cards, when actually the number was closer to $18,000. As one would expect, Eric was angry about the secret. Susan cried and explained that some of it came from extra expenses for the upcoming wedding. She promised to pay it off before they were married. He decided not to make an issue of it—after all, he loved her.

Susan admitted in therapy that even from the beginning she hid packages from Eric, removed price tags from new purchases, and told him things weren't new when they were. She had always secretly hoped that Eric, who was responsible about money, would help her control herself. Yet she had never told him the truth.

Susan was lucky that her husband challenged her to change. Desperate, she turned to the practical and psychological tools outlined in this book. In therapy, she took guidance and learned how to survive without credit cards. By keeping track of her purchases, she learned to be conscious about her spending. This discipline enabled her to develop a spending plan tailor-made for her lifestyle. Since then, Susan has created a vision of her dream life, and now she has the tools to accomplish her dreams. She's no longer reliant on material expressions to prove that she fits in. She's learned that her intrinsic value as a person resides inside, not in outer appearances. Most important, because she has clarity about her spending, she no longer needs to deceive herself or others.

A Cultural Problem

Susan is not unusual. She developed this problem because she lives in a culture that teaches outer appearances and material acquisitions can soothe psychological problems and enhance self-worth. Like Susan, most of us believe that others will accept us and think more highly of us if we have more stuff, or fancy stuff, or the latest stuff. Our psyches are marinated in promises of status and esteem gained through material possessions.

Large corporations implement highly sophisticated advertising campaigns convincing you that their products are necessary and will help you solve your problems. They first remind you of your human fallibility and personal insecurities, and then promise you redemption from your feelings of inadequacy or shame. Advertisements instill hope to achieve psychological states of being—like happiness, popularity, inner peace, sex appeal, and superiority to others—through particular products.

 LARGE CORPORATIONS IMPLEMENT HIGHLY SOPHISTICATED ADVERTISING CAMPAIGNS CONVINCING YOU THAT THEIR PRODUCTS ARE NECESSARY AND WILL HELP YOU SOLVE YOUR PROBLEMS.

Advertisers have studied your desires since you were a child, striving to gain brand or product loyalty from you. They have manipulated your desires by subtly and precisely targeting your fantasies. According to some sources, each day the average person is bombarded with an average of three thousand advertisements.[1] Each message is designed to influence and shape your values and preferences. These marketing techniques have taught you to over-identify with image and material possessions. Whereas people once thought, "I am what I *do*," they now believe, "I am what I *buy*."[2]

This is further complicated because we also live in a culture accustomed to using credit. Until the economic crisis of fall 2008, credit had become increasingly easy for everyone to acquire, and easy credit allows you to buy whatever your credit limit will allow. You can buy things without waiting until you have the money to buy them. Credit is instant and it's convenient. You can spend money without thinking whether you really need the item or even if you actually like it. Most important, you don't have to reflect on whether you can afford it, and often people don't reflect. Except in times of extreme economic turmoil, such as the 2008 recession, there are few barriers to credit in modern society because after the credit cards, there are home equity credit lines and refinancing.

Our media raised the bar for what is considered *average* or *normal* because they portray rich and lavish lifestyles as both desirable and within reach. Only a few generations ago, living within one's means in a paid-for modest home was an honorable achievement and a sign of success. However, modern cultural messages now convince you that you are inadequate if your possessions are merely *average.*

Technological advancements have altered our definition of *normal.* Everyone now expects new, newer, and newest when it comes to electronics. People believe they are missing out on life if they haven't upgraded to the latest flat screen TV, iPod, cell phone, camera, and so on. Perfectly functional items are quickly replaced with newer versions. With instant credit approval and instant financing, you can walk out of a car dealership with a new vehicle in a few hours. Even these major purchases are made without forethought or a budget. For the impulsive buyer, this dangerous system results in large car payments and financial self-destruction. Easy credit, offered under the guise of convenience, leads to overconsumption.

 WE HAVE MANY CULTURAL FORCES AT PLAY THAT ENCOURAGE US TO SPEND OUR MONEY, BUT WE HAVE FEW SKILLS TO MANAGE OUR MONEY. THE FINANCIAL PLANNING INDUSTRY CALLS THIS *FINANCIAL ILLITERACY.*

The sheer multitude of product choices in the American marketplace influences financial behavior. No longer do we choose between Keds and Converse when we need athletic shoes. Now we have many companies producing different shoes for specific uses—running, tennis, walking, indoor, hiking, and trail running, to name a few. Consumers are confused and overwhelmed by unending choices. With so many options to choose from, we believe we should be able to select and own the best of everything. Some people end up unsatisfied, always wondering if they made the right choice. These unlimited options lead to increased comparison with others, regret, and even unhappiness.[3]

THE TERMS I USE

Discussion about money problems is not new. However, the exploration of money use as a disorder, especially the possibility that money behaviors may be addictive, *is* new. I believe that money behaviors become addictive—deeply damaging and progressive—for some people. For many more, the problems remain deep and static or cyclical.

We tend to think of only two stereotyped problems related to money—the compulsive spender, shopping himself into ever-deeper debt, or the miserly hoarder, clinging to every penny while her children wear worn clothes.

But in real life, money problems are more complex and are expressed in many ways. For this reason, in this book I have chosen to use the phrase *people with money problems and money addiction* when referring to the cluster of behaviors that are symptoms of a problematic relationship with money. For convenience, I often use the phrase *problem users and money addicts* to describe these individuals.

In the course of this book, you will learn more about the types of money problems, how they can spiral into addiction, and how to recover from them.

We have many cultural forces at play that encourage us to spend our money, but we have few skills to manage our money. The financial planning industry calls this *financial illiteracy.* Research has revealed the obvious: Americans don't understand basic economic concepts and lack money management skills. This is troublesome, because money skills are increasingly complex. We rarely use tangible currency (cash) to fund our lives. We barely come into contact with real money because we have direct deposit of paychecks, online banking, and the use of plastic cards for payment. Because money is intangible, we don't witness how it flows into our lives as income and then flows out to pay for necessary expenses. Thus, concepts such as cash flow and budgeting are completely lost. Future-oriented financial skills like saving for retirement and investment decisions are out of range for an impulsive and financially illiterate society. Financial planners attempt to educate us by offering financial products and possibilities, but these complicated products can't help a person who doesn't understand how to prepare a simple budget.

Lack of financial education, coupled with the complexity of modern financial survival, is a fast formula for growing financial dysfunctions—a breeding ground for problems with money, spending, and self-control. It's no surprise that so many people have so much trouble with money management.

No wonder money problems are so prevalent in our culture.

How This Book Will Help

This book will help you understand your relationship with money. You will learn about many types of people with money troubles: people who spend too much (compulsive spenders), people who avoid money (money averters), and people who hoard money (hoarders). Some people have more serious problems than others. Some are slightly abnormal in their relationships to money, some have recurring but manageable problems, and others have severe and progressive—even addictive—problems. This book can help you regardless of your particular problem and regardless of the seriousness of your situation.

This book will help you understand *why* you do what you do and will outline tools for permanent change. If you tend to indulge yourself with money and material goods, you'll learn how to discipline yourself to live within your means. If you tend to deprive yourself (or others) or avoid money matters, this book will help you understand how to relate rationally to money. When you disentangle from materialistic avoidance or obsessions and preoccupations, you'll learn that money does not define you or bring you self-worth. You'll see that money is merely an instrument, a tool of exchange. The techniques in this book will enable you to use money in ways that are congruent with your values. You won't want to waste money because you'll want to spend it on things really important to you. Despite the culture around you and despite your family upbringing, you will learn to have your own healthy relationship with money.

 WHEN YOU DISENTANGLE FROM MATERIALISTIC AVOIDANCE OR OBSESSIONS AND PREOCCUPATIONS, YOU'LL LEARN THAT MONEY DOES NOT DEFINE YOU OR BRING YOU SELF-WORTH.

This book is divided into two parts. The first part will help you understand the ways in which money behaviors can be addictive, the emotional sources of money troubles, types of money problems, and their effect on relationships. The second part will show you how to put together and follow a plan to recover from your money problems or money addiction.

In chapter 2, we will use two models of alcohol addiction to demonstrate how money problems can grow into an addiction. We'll look at the range, from healthy to problematic to outright addictive money behaviors. We'll also take a look at how other psychological problems, like depression, attention deficit/ hyperactivity disorder (ADHD), and compulsive gambling, influence money behaviors.

In chapter 3, we'll explore the emotional roots of your current behavior with money. As we explore a multitude of life experiences (from childhood influences to generational trends), you'll begin to understand how complex our relationship with money really is.

Chapter 4 will outline the many different faces of problematic money behavior. We'll introduce you to the Money Problems Matrix, which centers around four quadrants of dysfunctional money behavior (spending, financial dependence, hoarding, and financial underachievement). Even if your problems are not severe, you'll probably recognize something of yourself and your loved ones in this analysis: some people deprive themselves of material pleasures, and some indulge themselves; some people obsess about money management, and others avoid it.

Chapter 5 will take a look at the very complicated role of money in relation-ships. You'll be introduced to the various ways in which people with different money styles relate to each other. You'll see how two indulgers relate to each other, how a depriver and an indulger relate, and how a healthy money manager relates to a troubled money manager.

The second part of the book will provide you with tools to change your life. Beginning with chapter 6, you'll take stock of your situation. Through a series of questionnaires, you'll be encouraged to reflect on your circum-stances. These questions help you examine your current money behaviors and how your past influences them.

Chapter 7 will offer beginning money management tools. This chapter will help you experiment with new behaviors in order to start the change process. You will learn to stop using credit cards, to organize your financial papers, and to keep track of all your spending.

Chapter 8 will offer more in-depth financial planning skills, such as creating your life vision and making a spending plan. You'll be taught practical methods for handling your cash flow, paying off your debts, and developing savings. You'll finally be able to successfully implement a spending plan or budget. If you have had a tendency to deprive or hoard, you'll learn the impor-tance of setting a plan and spending *up* to it.

Chapter 9 will aim to keep you motivated and will teach you how to change your thinking, feelings, and actions. You'll learn to identify conditions that trigger you and techniques for tackling self-destructive behaviors.

Finally, chapter 10 will allow you to see the myriad possibilities of self-worth and abundance once you are free of the negative behaviors and beliefs that connect self-worth to money. You now have tools for living in balance with money, finding authentic means to happiness and self-expression, and creating a unique lifestyle for yourself.

Whatever your relationship with money, it's possible to find freedom and peace of mind about it. This change requires effort on your part, but if you make the small gradual changes suggested in this book, it's impossible to fail. The Sufis have a saying: "Trust in God, but tie your camel." This book offers you the rope to secure your camel so it will be there when you need it to take you places. You'll learn to pay enough attention to your finances so you can live your life joyously. You'll discover how to shape a satisfying, meaningful life that is filled with inner riches. You'll discover greater connection to yourself and the world around you. You'll learn to appreciate that you *already* have enough and that you, yourself, have worth.

Come, join in.

• • •

The Slippery Slope from
Money Problems to Money Addiction

Popular media regularly report the grim facts about Americans' financial habits:

- Between 1989 and 2006, Americans' total credit card charges rose from about $69 billion a year to more than $1.8 trillion.[1]

- Total U.S. consumer debt (credit card plus other nonmortgage debt) reached $2.55 trillion at the end of 2007, up from $2.42 trillion at the end of 2006.[2]

- From 2004 to 2006, Americans took out $840 billion per year from their homes through sales, second mortgages, and home equity lines of credit.[3]

- The average student graduating from college has almost $20,000 in debt; the average credit card debt for 25- to 34-year-olds has increased 47 percent between 1989 and 2004. Nearly 20 percent of young people aged 18 to 24 are in "debt hardship," up from 12 percent in 1989.[4]

- Young adults (ages 25 to 34) now spend nearly one-fourth of their income on debt payments.[5]

- More than 1.6 million Americans filed for bankruptcy in 2003, as opposed to about 926,600 in 1995 and just under 570,000 in 1987.[6]

- Home foreclosures and late payments set records over the first three months of 2008 and are expected to keep rising. The percentage of mortgages that started the foreclosure process climbed to 6.3 percent from the previous high of 5.29 percent. Late payments rose to 22.07 percent from 20.02 percent, the previous high.[7]

- Americans' savings rates declined from 7 percent of disposable income in the 1980s to 3.5 percent of disposable income in the 1990s.[8] Since the early 1980s, the household saving rate has averaged only about 1.5 percent.[9]

- Among problem debtors serviced by Myvesta, a nonprofit financial health organization, debt increased from an average of $52,210 per family in 2002 to $77,036 in 2003.[10]

If these alarming statistics portrayed the rapid spread of physical disease, we'd call it an epidemic. The Centers for Disease Control would be conducting massive research. Public service announcements would appear in every media outlet.

But that's not happening. The psychological dysfunction stirring under the statistics is neglected.

Obviously, there's a real problem—a problem with debilitating emotional, material, and spiritual consequences for each individual and his or her loved ones. Despite the damage, the financial planning industry pays little attention. Nor have the medical and psychological professions recognized the degree of crisis. The banking and credit card industry also has not taken note, except to line its pockets with ever more stringent penalties for overdrafts, late payments, and over-the-limit fines.

But the facts do suggest something is very wrong. As a therapist who has worked with people who are deeply troubled by financial woes, I am convinced that the problem is a true disorder. It starts as a pattern of problems with money and financial matters, and for some people at least, it becomes an addiction on the level of other behavioral addictions, such as gambling and eating disorders.

To be sure, this book is aimed at readers who have serious money problems as well as those who might be called money addicts. The processes suggested here will help both. But it is important for every reader to understand the nature of addiction and to consider whether his or her problems have reached that level.

Let's start our examination of money problems and money addiction by reviewing the best known of all addictions—alcoholism.

In the 1920s, 1930s, and even into the 1970s, alcoholism was seen as a problem brought on by faulty information and poor willpower. People thought that if alcoholics just recognized they had a problem and got enough gumption, they'd quit.

The wise founders of Alcoholics Anonymous (AA) regarded alcoholism as a *disease of the spirit,* not a moral issue. Later, the medical field demonstrated physiological and epidemiological patterns in families and within ethnic groups. The growth of AA and the increased recognition of the medical model of alcoholism helped health care professionals and the general public perceive alcoholism as a disease. Lack of education and willpower were no longer considered the underlying driving cause of addiction. In fact, addiction counselors know that many alcoholics want to stop drinking. They *want* to recover. Alcoholics not only make promises to themselves about their behavior; they also make many attempts to control or stop their drinking. Addicts are painfully self-recriminating, self-conscious, and ashamed of their inability to stop. They are indeed powerless over their addiction.

Such powerlessness is at the heart of one simple definition of addiction: *the inability to stop continued use of a substance or behavior despite many negative consequences.*

Alcoholism is both chronic and progressive—that is, it is long-lasting and it gets worse over time. One of the symptoms of alcoholism is a strong need to drink despite negative consequences, such as serious job or health problems. Like other diseases, addictions have a predictable course and are influenced by both genetic (inherited) and environmental factors. The disease transcends race, religion, gender, and socioeconomic status. It has physiological, psychological, emotional, and spiritual components.

Today we face the same position with money problems and money addiction that we faced with alcoholism seventy years ago. Just as people tried to cure alcoholism by preaching to alcoholics about the misery of their condition, financial educators preach that a course of action prescribed by a financial adviser will improve the money addict's situation. They use charts, future projections, and elaborate computer printouts in an attempt to "cure" financial woes. They see the problem as one of self-indulgence or lack of willpower. They believe that reasoning, scaring, scolding, and preaching will be enough to help money addicts change their behaviors or help themselves.

Of course, many people who have money problems will change when provided information, a plan of action, and support to maintain the will to change. This is true for some people who abuse alcohol or other drugs from time to time: with the right education and incentives, they'll stop on their own. These people are not addicts—in this book, I call them *people with money problems* or *problem users*. Still, for a significant number, no amount of information or training, no plan books, budgets, or willpower can help. These people will continue an abusive relationship with money regardless of massive "doses" of such cures. They use money differently than most people do. They use it in a way that I am certain is addictive.

This book will outline how a person's use of money can be considered addictive, much in the same manner as alcohol, drugs, food, sex, and gambling. You'll see that money addiction follows a predictable trajectory, just as these other addictions do. You'll see that there are different types of money addicts. You'll get help identifying where you fall on the spectrum from having money problems to money addiction. Finally, you'll learn tools to help yourself.

Let's dig into more detail by looking at some clinical indicators that show how the use of money may be addictive for some people.

Criteria for Addictions

There are many similarities between money addiction and other addictions. Here, two sources will help us: information from Alcoholics Anonymous and *The Diagnostic and Statistical Manual of Mental Disorders,* fourth edition (DSM-IV), which is used by health care professionals in diagnosing disorders. The DSM-IV defines substance dependence as "a cluster of cognitive, behavioral and physiological symptoms indicating that the individual continues use of the substance despite significant substance-related problems."

A paraphrased list of the criteria for substance addiction set out in DSM-IV includes the following:

- Increased tolerance
- Withdrawal
- Use of more than was intended
- Unsuccessful efforts to cut down
- A great deal of time spent pursuing and concealing

- Dropping important activities
- Continued use despite negative consequences

Alcoholics Anonymous also lays out criteria for addiction, including these:

- Compulsive lying
- Loss of time and blackouts
- Increasingly lowered standards of morality
- Hitting bottom

Using the complete DSM-IV definition and anecdotal criteria laid out by Alcoholics Anonymous for addiction, we'll see how for some people, money-related behaviors fit the profile of an addiction. (This comparison is summarized in charts 2-1 on page 17 and 2-2 on page 20.)

DSM-IV Criteria

INCREASED TOLERANCE

The DSM-IV defines tolerance as "the need for greatly increased amounts of the substance to achieve intoxication (or the desired effect) or a markedly diminished effect with continued use of the same amount of the substance." [11] If you are a problem user or a full-blown money addict, you may have intense pleasure in new purchases. But over time the pleasure doesn't last as long. You start fantasizing about your next purchase immediately after the last one, thinking ahead to when you'll have money to buy it. However, when more money *does* become available—for example, when your income increases—you spend beyond that new income level. This increased tolerance is obvious when people spend to their maximum credit card limit, increase their credit card balances, accumulate balances on several credit cards, and then take equity out of their homes. Their nonchalance or comfort level about increasing debt is a good indicator of increased tolerance.

WITHDRAWAL

The DSM-IV defines withdrawal as "a maladaptive behavioral change, with physiological and cognitive concomitants, that occurs when blood or tissue concentrations of a substance decline in an individual who had maintained prolonged heavy use of the substance. After developing unpleasant withdrawal symptoms, the person is likely to take the substance to relieve or avoid those symptoms."[12] Because money is not ingested, you won't experience physiological withdrawal. However, if you repeatedly use the substance to "relieve or avoid symptoms," you are likely to experience emotional withdrawal symptoms. If for some reason you have to stop making purchases, the withdrawal shows up as anxiety or restlessness or feeling inferior to other people. You feel pain and loss about not having the latest item or about not being able to visit your favorite stores. You typically feel jealous and agitated when others get new things. This panic of withdrawal is alleviated only when you purchase something new.

USE OF MORE THAN WAS INTENDED

Even normal money managers sometimes go to the store and purchase more than they intended. If you are a problem user, this behavior is more extreme. It is "normal" for you to buy more than you intended. You set limits on your spending, but you can't stay within your budget. You never intend to spend more than you earn, but somehow you always end up in debt. You don't intend to go over your credit limit, but an unusual situation always comes up.

 IF YOU ARE AN ADDICT, YOU TRULY CANNOT CONTROL YOUR BEHAVIOR. YOU WAKE UP EACH DAY PROMISING YOURSELF AND OTHERS THAT YOU WILL STOP. INEVITABLY YOU BREAK THE PROMISES.

In every case, you spend spontaneously. You tell yourself, it's just this one thing, this one time. No matter what you do, it's hard for you to stick to any sort of limit on yourself: not holiday budgets, vacation budgets, or kids' school clothes budgets. You really intend to use your credit cards only for emergencies, but inevitably something catches your eye. Credit tools enable you to spend more than you would if paying by cash. Clearly, "using more than intended" is a major feature for people with money problems and for money addicts.

UNSUCCESSFUL EFFORTS TO CUT DOWN

Addicts try repeatedly to modify their behaviors, and fail. If you are an addict, you truly cannot control your behavior. You wake up each day promising yourself and others that you will stop. Inevitably you break the promises. Seeing a sale that you can't pass up, or having a bad day at work, sets you off. You keep attempting to control yourself with simple control methods, such as freezing the credit cards in ice or limiting yourself to only on-sale or cheap items. Sometimes you may even be able to set aside money for a specific purpose. Occasionally, you are able to string some successes together and pay off a few debts and close out accounts. But eventually the addiction creeps in again, and you deplete any savings you did manage to accumulate, then reopen the accounts and accrue additional balances. These unsuccessful efforts demonstrate the addict's powerlessness over money.

A GREAT DEAL OF TIME SPENT PURSUING AND CONCEALING

As problems progress, more and more time is spent planning for the next high. As you become more preoccupied with the acquisition and use of your "drug of choice," the rest of life fades into the background. When the problem is money addiction, you spend time thinking about your purchases—perusing catalogs or Sunday newspaper advertisements—and then shopping for these items. You spend time communicating with the bank regarding bounced checks and late fee fines. Because you are always short on cash, you spend time juggling money online or making extra trips to the bank so as to not bounce checks. Financial obsessions are secretive, so you probably expend a lot of time and energy fielding creditor phone calls and intercepting the family mail.

DROPPING IMPORTANT ACTIVITIES

As preoccupation with an addiction grows, an addict's world becomes more insular. When money is your only meaningful activity, you stop deriving satisfaction or pleasure from nonmaterial experiences. You give up your lunch hour at work to go online with eBay. Saturdays are spent at the mall. You spend less time with family members and start to believe that shopping with your children is quality time with them. Usually you fantasize about material acquisitions and prefer activities that cost money. You are unable to consider experiences that don't cost money. Your hobbies center on spending money and include activities such as visiting the mall, dealing antiques, acquiring collectibles, or buying electronics and sports equipment. For example, you may have more interest in researching and buying technological gadgets for your nature photography hobby than in actually taking photographs.

CONTINUED USE DESPITE NEGATIVE CONSEQUENCES

A common feature of every addiction is denial of a problem and not seeing the negative consequences of our actions. Some people with money problems—and all money addicts—cannot see that they are digging themselves into a hole. With increased use, you ignore consequences of your behavior and manage to avoid situations that would cause you to see your circumstances for what they are. You can't stop, even though your behavior has caused troubles not just in your finances, but also with your partner and other relationships. If you are a problem user, you won't change your money habits even if your partner is angry and overworks to pay debts. You ignore the problem even if the depression, worry, and anxiety keep you up at night and your health starts to suffer.

You can't see the financial consequences, either. Your behavior costs extra money in late fees and interest charges, but you overlook that fact. Whether you pile the bills neatly or scatter them throughout the house, you manage to avoid opening them and looking at them. You duck out of phone calls from creditors, or if by chance creditors catch you off guard, you make the infamous promise, "The check is in the mail." You have every intention to keep your promises and really do believe you can pay those bills. However, like every addict, you distort your capabilities to solve the problem. Because you can't really see the problem, you make little real effort to change.

Addicts continue to use their substance of choice because they truly believe it is under control and really isn't that bad. This denial makes addicts less and less able to see how their financial behavior affects their financial reality. If you are in this category, you may find yourself unable to see the connection between today's spending habits and tomorrow's shortage of cash to pay for necessities like car repairs. Money addicts are unwilling to see the devastating consequences of their behavior until a bottom is reached.

The "size" or degree of denial is one of the differences between people with money problems—the majority of readers of this book—and money addicts. When you are on your way to addiction, you come in and out of denying your situation. Yet you are still able to self-correct because you can see your problem. Those moments of clarity diminish as you become a full-blown addict and your defenses grow.

Chart 2-1 summarizes the comparison between the DSM-IV features of substance dependence and the features observed in money addicts.

CHART 2-1

Is Money Addictive? A Look at DSM-IV Criteria

Features of Substance Dependence (DSM-IV)[13]	What This Feature Looks Like for a Money Addict
Increased tolerance	Addict constantly craves for more things and newer things. Spending exceeds income even as income increases. Overall debt increases over time. Addict's credit card bills grow, number of cards increases. Uses home equity and second mortgages as bailouts.
Withdrawal	Addict feels agitated, bored, or restless unless spending or shopping.
Use of more than was intended	Addict cannot keep to shopping list or budget. Goes over any preplanned budget (holidays, vacation, birthday presents).
Unsuccessful efforts to cut down	Addict tries not to shop; may cut up cards; breaks promises to self and others; may switch to Internet shops or limit stores frequented. May attempt control by returning items or getting home equity to pay off and start fresh, then ends up with home equity payment and new credit card charges.
A great deal of time spent pursuing and concealing	Addict browses catalogs, the Internet, or the mall. Spends increasing time juggling money from one account to another. May spend a lot of time shopping and returning items. Spends time researching or obsessing about purchases.
Dropping important activities	Addict makes shopping the major recreational activity. Believes shopping is a hobby.
Continued use despite negative consequences	Addict sees neither the problem nor the consequences. Can't stop even when under financial pressure or when bills are due. Keeps at it even if worry about paying bills causes anxiety, depression, and sleepless nights.

Alcoholics Anonymous Criteria

COMPULSIVE LYING

Addicts conceal the problem from partners, family, and friends. If you are in trouble with your financial behaviors, you probably hide any evidence of the situation from others. You stash purchases in the trunk of the car, in the back of the closet, at another's home, or at the office to deceive your partner. If challenged, you take tags off purchases or deny that an item is new. You make sure to be present at home to intercept the mail before your partner has access to it. If this isn't possible, you arrange for your mail to be delivered to another's home or you open a post office box. In the extreme, some addicts resort to elaborate deceptive bookkeeping and falsify financial statements so their partners won't know the truth about their spending.

LOSS OF TIME AND BLACKOUTS

The loss of time and consciousness while participating in addiction is a common theme from Alcoholics Anonymous. If you are a money addict, you "forget" the due dates of your bills, don't know what your overall expenses are, or lose track of how much money you have in your bank account. You can't remember which bills are already paid and which ones aren't. You mysteriously space out and can't understand where your money has disappeared to. After shopping, you sometimes don't remember what you bought. You're even surprised when you come home and realize that you have purchased a duplicate of something you already own. You lose track of time while shopping and remain in a store much longer than you intended. Money addicts live in a vague reality about finances and are often unable to account for where the money goes.

INCREASINGLY LOWERED STANDARDS OF MORALITY

Addiction in its advanced state causes a person to lose sight of his or her values and to lose moral parameters. Addicts decline into self-destructive behavior. Under pressure, money addicts lie on time cards, embezzle from employers, or participate in illegal and immoral activities, such as coercing family members with fewer resources to lend money. Increasingly desperate for money to pay the bills, addicts turn to high-interest predators or illegal sources, such as loan sharks. A full-blown addict stops at nothing. He or she feels compelled to use dishonest schemes to get money from grown children or elderly parents, using others' homes as collateral.

HITTING BOTTOM

Addictions demand increased consumption, get worse over time, and burn through every possible limitation, but eventually a bottom is reached. At this bottoming-out point, the consequences are impossible to ignore. Painful realities overtake the fantasy of sustaining the habit. For alcoholics and drug addicts, the body and soul pay a toll. If you are a money addict, the bottom comes when you have exhausted all avenues to borrow money and can no longer juggle payments and current bills. Backed into a corner, you can't sustain the illusion of financial fitness. Because you're unable to see the real problem, you can't see any solutions, either. With no money to fuel your habit, you have no fantasy to soothe yourself. You have nowhere to go. You experience a painful withdrawal caused by the cessation of spending and charging as well as your shattered illusions of material wealth. Previous delusions and self-deceptions prove to be hollow when you face the emptiness inside both your bank account and yourself. This is the bottom, and it hurts.

At the bottom, addicts are flooded with many difficult emotions, such as anxiety, panic, fear, dread, despair, and hopelessness. Remember, without the substance of choice, addicts have limited coping strategies. Panic sets in upon recognition of the extent of the mess. Much like people facing the aftermath of a fire or flood, addicts are in a kind of shock and can't imagine where to begin. Faced with equally urgent bills and financial responsibilities, the situation seems insurmountable. For some addicts the solution is through a quick fix or escape through bankruptcy. For others suicide looms as a seemingly logical choice.

Chart 2-2, on the next page, summarizes the parallels between descriptions of addiction in AA and common behaviors of money addiction.

Deprivation Money Addiction

So far, we've focused strictly on the traditional overindulgent model of addiction based on alcoholism. However, unlike the use of alcohol, spending money is necessary on a daily basis for survival. Some people have a problematic relationship to money or a money addiction that manifests in a form that is difficult to recognize—deprivation. Deprivation isn't a form of addiction with alcohol, because doing without alcohol isn't detrimental to survival. *Deprivation money addiction* occurs when a person becomes obsessed with holding onto money and with constraining spending of any sort. These deprivers go beyond

19

CHART 2-2

Is Money Addictive? A Look at Alcoholics Anonymous Addiction Characteristics

Characteristics of Addiction (Alcoholics Anonymous)	What This Feature Looks Like for a Money Addict
Compulsive lying	Addict lies to partner and/or asks partner to lie to creditors. Says everything is great and gives impression of being successful.
Loss of time and blackouts	Addict loses track of time while participating in addictive activity. Forgets what already owns, so purchases duplicates. Is confused and unclear about financial agreements.
Increasingly lowered standards of morality	Addict's debt leads to stealing or embezzling. Takes relatives' money, even children's.
Hitting bottom	Partner finds out about the behaviors. All avenues for borrowing money are exhausted. Savings and retirement funds are depleted. Home is repossessed. Homelessness may follow.

thriftiness and deprive themselves of material security and comfort through overcontrolled spending. Deprivation addiction manifests as either an obsession about the accumulation of money or total avoidance of financial matters. This deprivation is similar to an eating-disordered or anorexic individual who avoids eating food despite the fact that food is necessary for survival. Money deprivers pride themselves on not spending money, even if they have money in the bank. Self-deprivation can have dire consequences on family relationships when the depriver expects others to do without or when they control family relationships by withholding money.

A Continuum of Money Behaviors

Addictions exist on a continuum that ranges from good health to problem use to full-scale dependence and addiction. This range is true for both substance addictions (alcohol, drugs, food) and behavioral addictions (sex, gambling, money).

This continuum is more difficult to discern in money addiction, because money is essential to contemporary life, and every adult has to use it regularly, often daily. Alcohol and drugs are peripheral to human subsistence, being used primarily for medicinal or recreational purposes. Hence, if a person is slipping down the slope of chemical addiction, it's obvious that he or she needs to stop chemical use altogether in order to recover. (Unless, of course, the person has a health condition that requires the use of a mood-altering drug.) But, because money is essential for modern-day survival, it's more complicated to tease true money addictions from the larger sphere of financial problems. Personal finances do not remain static; they constantly fluctuate with different life circumstances. Thus, it is not uncommon to have periods in an individual's lifespan when finances may be tight; at such a time, loans and credit cards can be helpful tools. Some people deal with their finances in healthy, normal ways; others regularly misuse financial tools and money in troubled ways; and some are full-blown money addicts. The following sections will help you recognize behaviors along this continuum.

A Healthy Relationship with Money

Healthy people respect money. Healthy people spend money consciously and with discipline. If you have a healthy relationship with money, you recognize that there are financial limits and you know how to honor them. You follow the rules of money. This means you take care of your material needs while living within the limits of your income. You may follow a plan or budget for spending. Sometimes you splurge on a special gift for yourself, but then return to a balance point either by paying it off over time or waiting to make additional purchases until you have replenished your reserves.

For example, while on vacation in Europe, John purchased a $5,000 watch. Prior to the trip, he had been interested in this manufacturer and satisfied his curiosity by pricing them in local jewelry stores. He did not intend to buy the watch on his vacation. However, while in Europe, he saw the watch offered at a reasonable price and decided to dip into his reserves and purchase the watch. Over the course of the next six months, he did not allow himself to spend frivolously or to take another vacation until his savings reserves had been replaced.

Healthy money managers like John can delay gratification, save for high-ticket items, and resist purchases they can't afford. If you are a healthy money manager, you can tolerate your inner desires without acting on them, even when you see others around you purchase these items. You understand that material objects do not bring happiness, and you enjoy what you already own. You may experience temporary short-term financial pinches, but because you remain conscious about finances, you quickly self-correct.

Healthy deprivers live frugally. They don't look for validation from materialism or status. Rather than indulging themselves materially, they give to charity and use their money for others. Such people may make do with less than others, but they aren't unhappy about money or trying to hoard it or avoid its use. They simply choose to live with less; constitutionally, they may have fewer needs than the norm or may make the choice out of a well-reasoned principle.

A Problematic Relationship with Money

People with money problems (or *problem users*) have started on the path to addiction. In most cases, spending money makes these people happy—and that happiness supersedes logic. If you have a problematic relationship to money, you'll charge items without knowing how you will pay for them. Your income is able to withstand the damage you do on your credit cards, because you don't necessarily carry high debt loads and are usually able to get the balance down to zero in a year or two. You may also hold the zero balance for a period of time. These spending splurges represent temporary denial of total expenses, but eventually you're able to get back on solid financial ground. You probably don't have a large savings reserve to help you through difficult times or emergencies, but you can manage because your debt is not overly large.

 IF YOU HAVE A PROBLEMATIC RELATIONSHIP TO MONEY, YOU'LL CHARGE ITEMS WITHOUT KNOWING HOW YOU WILL PAY FOR THEM.

The problem user slips in and out of reality about the facts of his or her financial situation. If you are such a person, sometimes you can see the problem for what it is, and sometimes you can't. Sometimes you break the rules, and other times you remember your financial limits. Just like a dieter who loses twenty pounds over and over again every three to four years, the problem money manager has a self-imposed limit for how far he or she will get off track. Whether that limit is the available credit on one credit card or a specific dollar comfort zone, he or she is able to curtail spending in order to restore reserves.

This person is on a slippery slope to addiction.

The *problematic depriver* is beginning to be preoccupied with saving money and self-restraint in spending. He or she may occasionally avoid necessary home repairs or miss paying a bill out of a desire to avoid spending. Material deprivation is beginning to influence lifestyle choices and decisions about spending, but it has not become addictive. He or she may also be embarking on a path of underemployment as a part of the deprivation.

The Addictive Relationship to Money

Just as some problem drinkers become alcoholics, so too do some problem spenders become full-blown money addicts. For the money addict, problem spending grows worse over time until the behavior becomes an out-of-control addiction in its own right. If you are a money addict, you do not respect financial limits. When you hit the maximum credit limit, you simply acquire a second, third, or ninth card, and you request increased credit limits. You borrow from friends and family. You have no internal controls and are unable to heed external limitations.

Over time addictions destroy lives. If you have a money addiction, it affects every relationship you have—with family, friends, and business. Promises to self and others are repeatedly broken. A money addiction prompts an individual to spend recklessly and without regard for the needs of loved ones; for example, children's medical needs can be neglected. Because of the stress caused by constant anxiety about money, decision-making ability and physical health are also compromised.

Ultimately this altered state of reality will destroy personal integrity and happiness. In an advanced stage, you will lose all sense of moral obligation, possibly violating others' financial boundaries, even resorting to stealing. Your false sense of power prevents you from identifying what is wrong. If you don't know what the problem is, you have no idea what needs to change. Money addicts are powerless over the addiction. In a progressed state, every type of addict is extremely self-destructive, and some resort to suicide.

Addictive deprivers view acquisition of money as the primary object of their life. Their world is increasingly confined to focus on their finances. Their deprivation alienates and frustrates family members and those around them.

Some Examples

We all have to use money to live, and often to purchase things that will bring us pleasure. So let's look now at how people with healthy, problematic, and addictive relationships to money approach everyday activities: shopping, budgeting, managing debt, saving, and investing.

BEHAVIOR: SHOPPING

• *Healthy*

You buy what you need. You research purchases ahead of time and wait until you are able to purchase exactly what you want. You go to the store with a list and come home with only those items.

• *Problematic*

You are inconsistent with planning for purchases. Sometimes you can stick to a shopping list; other times you stretch the list. It happens spontaneously and without forethought. For example, the salesperson was persuasive, you are jealous because your coworker was offered a promotion, or your children pushed particularly hard for something. The erratic shopping habit leaves you short of cash for necessary expenses and results in long-term damage to the overall family finances. You use shopping to make yourself feel better, rather than using more direct solutions (such as resolving the problem that is causing discomfort). The *depriver shopper* has a hard time letting go of money, and this may cause various problems. For example, the depriver delays or makes a fuss about necessary purchases such as school supplies, even though there's enough money, leaving his or her children feeling deprived, abnormal, and neglected.

• *Addictive*

You frequently shop to reduce stress, numb feelings, and regulate emotions. You buy on impulse. Life is centered on acquisition shopping or shopping for recreation. You purchase duplicates of items, unable to remember what you already have. When shopping, *depriver addicts* won't buy basic necessities, fearing that spending money will leave them vulnerable.

BEHAVIOR: SHORT- AND LONG-TERM BUDGETING

- *Healthy*

  You spend within a long-term budget, spend consciously on what is needed, and recognize the reality that tomorrow's needs impact today's financial choices.

- *Problematic*

  You are able to stay within a long-term budget, especially if your partner or employer helps you save, but you have difficulty keeping to a short-term budget. You can't budget for large-ticket items. The *problematic depriver* creates extremely constrained budgets that are difficult to adhere to.

- *Addictive*

  You see no need for budgeting, have no financial goals, and focus exclusively on immediate bills and expenses. The *depriver addict* denies him- or herself necessities in order to focus solely on keeping the budget, so as to alleviate fears about the future.

BEHAVIOR: MANAGING DEBT

- *Healthy*

  You usually pay off credit card balances monthly and only rarely carry a balance.

- *Problematic*

  You usually pay the entire balance of your debts. Occasionally you leave a balance that adds interest to the debt. After building the debt for a set period of time or amount, you are eventually able to get the debt load down to a zero balance. If the *problematic depriver* does accumulate debt, he or she focuses on paying off debt, even mortgage debt, to the exclusion of other expenses, such as children's orthodontics or a pleasurable vacation.

- *Addictive*

  You acquire larger and larger debts. You allow late fees and increased interest expenses to accrue. You increase overall debt load by borrowing against equity lines. You have few financial boundaries to limit debt load. The *addictive depriver* has an extreme aversion to debt and is fearful of the vulnerability of owing money. He or she feels morally superior in having no debt.

BEHAVIOR: SAVING

• *Healthy*

You have diverse savings; these savings are part of the everyday budget.

• *Problematic*

You can save for midterm goals but not for long-term goals. You will tend to dip into savings to satisfy immediate splurges. The *problematic depriver* focuses on savings, finding it easy to do without things in the present. He or she prefers to decline pleasurable activities while deriving satisfaction from saving money.

• *Addictive*

You have no savings or constantly deplete any reserves you do accumulate. You deplete 401(k) or retirement plans or borrow from family or children's savings. The *depriver addict* is exclusively focused on saving money as the primary goal in life, sacrificing all other needs.

BEHAVIOR: INVESTING

• *Healthy*

You make investments as part of a long-term savings strategy. You employ professionals and educate yourself about finances.

• *Problematic*

You hold scattered or undeveloped investments and borrow against investments. The *problem depriver* has begun to derive a sense of emotional safety through investments.

• *Addictive*

You hold no investments, or have entirely depleted your own and often others' resources. The *depriver addict* may have massive accumulation of investments and an addictive preoccupation with tracking the stock market.

When Money Addiction Overlaps with Other Conditions

With many psychological conditions, a constellation of symptoms that appears to be characteristic of one particular disorder often overlaps with those of another. Addictions often mimic other disorders at first glance, making it especially challenging to develop a clear and accurate diagnosis. Put another way, it can be difficult to tell if a behavior is the root problem or a symptom of some other problem. This is certainly true for money-related behaviors. While this is not a book about diagnosis of mental health problems, it is helpful for you to know some of the other conditions that can accompany or exacerbate money addiction. As a therapist, I have seen many common mental illnesses along with (or disguised as) money-related addictive behaviors. Sometimes a mental disorder is the actual problem, and other times the psychological problems occur in tandem with problematic money behaviors.

Attention Deficit/Hyperactivity Disorder (ADHD)

Many ADHD behaviors mimic money addiction. A person with ADHD may make impulsive purchases, have such disorganized financial records that they lose bills and bounce checks, underachieve with both career and finances, and have math or other learning disorders. Here, you (with a therapist) need to determine if there is a real money addiction going on or if ADHD is at work. As a therapist, I have seen people with ADHD who have major money problems not because they were problem users or full-blown addicts, but because their ADHD manifested itself as dysfunctional financial behavior. Resolution of the ADHD helped improve the money behaviors.

Bipolar Affective Disorder (BAD)

The manic phase of bipolar affective disorder commonly leads to excessive spending. In this phase, the individual's financial judgment is so impaired that the person spends money recklessly. These unrestrained spending binges often involve large amounts of money in a very short period of time.

Gambling Addiction

People commonly confuse money addiction with gambling addiction. Gambling is its own addiction. This person has financial problems *because* he or she has used household money or credit cards to fund an expensive addiction. Gamblers bet on uncertain outcomes and become addicted to the arousal from intermittent wins or rewards. Compulsive gamblers fantasize that the wagers will bring money and provide them with a luxurious lifestyle. In contrast, a person who has a problematic relationship with money lacks money because he or she either spends it unconsciously or simply doesn't earn enough to live on.

Both gamblers and money addicts mistakenly believe they have a financial problem, not an emotional problem or addiction. Both mistakenly believe more money will solve their problem, when most often more money would only escalate the spending or gambling. No amount is ever enough for an addict. If untreated, both addictions culminate in dire financial circumstances. However, the two addictions are distinct and require different treatment strategies. A spending addict treated for gambling addiction would show no improvement, just as a gambling addict treated for money addiction would continue to gamble.

Depression

Debt and money problems can contribute to, as well as result from, depression. Individuals who are depressed are unable to sustain the necessary effort to improve their financial circumstances or may overspend in an attempt to lift their spirits. They may avoid important financial tasks, such as opening and paying bills and depositing paychecks. Serious money problems also cause depression, though the depression often recedes as the finances improve.

Generalized Anxiety Disorder (GAD)

Individuals suffering from generalized anxiety disorder may shop as a means to reduce anxiety and to avoid difficult life decisions and circumstances. Also, debt and financial difficulties are stressful and may actually cause anxiety. This anxiety interferes with daily life through panic attacks, insomnia, or heart palpitations.

Obsessive-Compulsive Disorder (OCD)

Individuals suffering from OCD look like money addicts—either spenders or deprivers—but are actually suffering from an anxiety disorder. They obsess over, shop for, and collect "perfect" items. These individuals may hoard money or possessions and be unable to throw away old worn objects.

Shoplifting or Kleptomania

Shoplifting is an impulse control disorder. Shoplifters often have adequate finances and act on the impulse to steal things they don't need. They feel "tension before the theft" and "pleasure, gratification, or relief when committing the theft."[14] The pleasurable feeling is its own reward; the shoplifter is not expressing some other emotion such as anger, and typically is able to afford the things he or she has stolen.

Antisocial Personality Disorder

Antisocial personality disorder was formerly called sociopathy. According to the DSM-IV, these disturbed individuals have no conscience about "conning others for personal profit or pleasure."[15] They cheat or steal from others without remorse. They are candidates for embezzlement and investment scams and theft. Their behavior doesn't grow out of a money addiction, although it looks like one. Because they fail to conform to social norms, they often end up in the criminal justice system.

As you can see, money addictions are easily tangled with other conditions. Therefore, seek professional help to discern which disorder is the primary culprit causing your behavior. *Never rush to diagnose either yourself or your loved ones.* If a person does indeed suffer from a money addiction and it is not properly addressed, the root cause of other behaviors may be misunderstood and inadequately treated.

Summary

When assessed in light of the commonly accepted definitions of addiction, money-related dysfunctions certainly fall into that category. For the problem user or money addict, "Some is not enough and more demands more." The surprise is that specialists in the field of addiction and substance abuse treatment hadn't reached this conclusion sooner.

• • •

The Emotional Sources
of Money Problems

In the previous chapter, we learned about various manifestations of money problems and money addiction. This chapter will address the *roots* of dysfunctional behavior around finances, even when the behavior is not yet addictive.

In my practice, I've observed that several categories of childhood experiences are shared by people with money problems and money addictions. I've divided these into factors that occur *within* the home (for example, having parents who are money addicts, the experience of severe trauma, and inborn characteristics) and factors *outside* the home (social influences such as the generation a person was born in or media influences).

Before we explore these, let's consider the case of Jack, a client with severe troubles whom I eventually came to realize was a money addict. When Jack was six, his father divorced his alcoholic mother, with whom Jack remained. Because his mother spent much of the child support money at the bar, she was unable to provide basic necessities such as regular groceries. At age ten, Jack began earning money to pay for food and some school activities. He worked hard, and his friend's parents provided some transportation for him. In high school, a teacher urged him to apply for scholarships to college. Jack went to college and went on to become a highly successful businessman. For the past ten years, his annual income has varied from $400,000 to $800,000 depending on bonuses from the business. As an adult, he has been unable to stop lavish spending, despite his accountant's yearly admonishments about the credit card balances. He claims he likes to have successful people as friends. He also likes highly visible items—jewelry, couture clothing, and a prominent winter vacation home. Jack worries that he will one day be back where he came from as a child. Now in his late sixties, Jack has borrowed equity out of his homes and has little savings. Savings would possibly help him feel more secure, but his addiction ensures that he will indeed end up in circumstances similar to his childhood.

From his case, you can clearly see how certain childhood factors set the stage for Jack's eventual problems, and ultimately his addiction to spending. Let's look in detail at the effect of childhood experiences on our relationship with money.

How Family Influences Money Behaviors

A great number of things may have happened in your family of origin to pre-dispose you to have money problems as an adult. Some of these factors over-lap, some set in motion a chain of causation, and some occur simultaneously. They are not neat categories, but seeing them as categories can help you think about your own experiences and whether they may have set you up for later problems with money. These familial factors include:

- Childhood trauma
- A financially stressed childhood
- Parents with money addictions
- Begrudging parents
- Parental conflicts about money
- Innate and learned preferences

As an adult, distinguishing between these groupings helps you trace historical causes for your money problems. But children are unable to make distinctions between these events. Children feel events without the benefit of explanations that help them understand, so they tend to experience them at a much deeper level than do adults. Children also have little or no control over events, and so are more vulnerable to their impact. Children depend on parents for emotional support and physical survival. If either of these dependence needs is not adequately and freely met, children will not trust their parents to take care of them. For example, if your parents had lost their home due to financial cir-cumstances, as a child you might not have totally trusted that your parents would figure out a way to get another home. Even if your parents were fully responsible and *did* find another home, as a child you probably simply felt afraid. You couldn't comprehend that your parents would take care of you and were indeed capable of making the necessary financial decisions. If your parents didn't have the ability to relay messages of safety during stressful times, you may have been left with long-standing insecure feelings about physical survival.

Let's look at each of these family events in turn.

Childhood Trauma

Leslie is a clear example of how numerous childhood traumas affect adult financial behavior. Leslie came to therapy after her husband found out that she owed $35,000 on credit cards, and because of this she realized that she had become a compulsive spender. She reported during therapy that her father had sexually abused her when she was a child, and that her mother and father fought constantly about money. She described how special she felt when her father came home with presents for her and how her mother flew into jealous rages over the gifts. After high school graduation, Leslie married a man who became very successful in business and kept tight control on her spending. Her compulsive spending kicked in when she had children and began to buy extravagant gifts for them. Over the course of therapy it became clear that buying the gifts for her children was the way that Leslie medicated the sexual abuse she experienced as a child.

 IN MONEY ADDICTION, TRAUMA IS BY FAR THE MOST POWERFUL UNDERLYING INFLUENCE.

It is widely accepted in the trauma treatment field that childhood trauma (sexual abuse, physical abuse, emotional abuse, and extreme neglect) predisposes a person to addictive behavior. In her book *Trauma and Addiction,* therapist Tian Dayton explains that a person who is abused develops defensive strategies to avoid feeling emotional pain from the abuse. These strategies include self-medication with chemicals, behavioral addictions, or both. These affect the pleasure centers of the brain and alter brain chemistry. She writes, "This means of handling trauma can lead to the disease of addiction."[1] Other specialists in addiction concur. Addictions serve to repeat the trauma and also to imitate adult behavior, both well-recognized behavior patterns in trauma victims.

In money addiction, trauma is by far the most powerful underlying influence. Because money is central to survival, childhood abuse and threats to your physical safety and security predispose you to money addictions as an adult. As an adult, you'll tend to either (a) fear material security and comfort or (b) pursue wealth relentlessly.

In the first instance—the person who fears security and comfort—the adult *repeats the early insecurity and trauma* through avoidance of or fear of material security and comfort. As adults, they use passivity to cope, just as they did as children. In doing so, the trauma survivor is unable to separate from abusive caretakers. This loyalty keeps them attached to the early experience of insecurity and powerlessness. In adulthood, money is their arena of powerlessness. Their adult financial behaviors repeat and ensure the beliefs from their childhood: *The world isn't safe, I can never be safe, and I want nothing to do with security of any sort.*

Those people in the second category—those who pursue financial security at any cost—are attempting to run from or assuage the early trauma. Here, the trauma has left the victim feeling virtually powerless.

The pursuit of money is a way of proving to the self that he or she is free from abusive caretakers. As an adult, the person unconsciously believes that money is power and will protect him or her. Because the person feels unable to trust or depend on others, money and possessions become his or her security. The belief system says, *The world is not safe; I cannot depend on others; I must have money (or status or image) to ensure my safety.*

Financially Stressed Childhood

Financial circumstances in the childhood home also set the stage for a troubled relationship with money. If your past included such stressors, *difficult financial circumstances can leave you either overvaluing or undervaluing money.* These difficult financial circumstances may have ripped your family apart, leaving you to fend for yourself before an appropriate age. In some cases, you may have come to believe that material success solves problems. As an adult, you may be confused about money, either paralyzed around money or obsessed with its pursuit. Because an infusion of additional money in your household may have solved some problems for your family, you may perceive money as the primary solution to problems.

While we typically think of financial stress as caused by poverty, stress exists in homes with extreme wealth as well. This can result in either over-valuing wealth or actively rebelling against the importance of money. Too much money and overindulgence can sometimes result in an adult who doesn't know how to handle money, doesn't respect money, or worships money. None of these are healthy ways to relate to money.

For example, Elaine's mother bought her everything she wanted as a child. Birthdays and holidays often involved twenty-five or more gifts. As an adult, Elaine is unable to stick to the budget her husband has prepared for them. She is unwilling to look at their current financial circumstances. She does not recognize the strain that her *learned* self-indulgent behavior puts on her husband.

Parents with Money Addictions

Your parents' *specific financial behaviors* are another contributor to money addictions, particularly if either of your parents was a full-blown money addict. If your parents were out of control and unable to manage the finances, it's likely that their behavior affected your relationship with money. It's even more likely that they denied that their behavior had an impact on you. For example, parents' impulsive overspending may result in financial deprivation of their children's basic needs and may even force the children into prematurely taking on the financial and emotional responsibilities of the dysfunctional parent. The parent may use the grocery money to buy another pair of new shoes or pay exorbitant dues for a country club and then tell the children that there isn't enough money for college. The children don't learn the appropriate use of money to meet practical needs. On a deeper level, the children learn that their practical needs are not as important as their parents' wants. This results in children who may feel guilty because they have learned that their own needs deprive their parents. If this conflict isn't resolved, children will not learn a healthy relationship to money and will be predisposed to money addiction.

Many adult financial behaviors are simple imitations of parental behavior. If you were taken along while your mother shopped when she was depressed, you learned that shopping is a way to medicate unpleasant feelings—and in the process, you learned to see money as soothing. If you witnessed a parent's financial dishonesty—lying to your other parent, to the credit card company, or to your siblings—you grew up to believe that such behavior is normal. You may have grown up seeing bounced checks, automobile repossession, or even bankruptcy as a normal part of life. You may have answered the phone and received the dunning calls from creditors or witnessed a parent's illegal activities for money. You may have watched your parents flaunting material success, or at the other extreme, hoarding and hiding their material success from others. Even if your parents were not full-blown addicts themselves, their financial behaviors left an embarrassing mark. For example, perhaps they argued with your piano teacher in front of you about the cost of the books or overdue lesson payments, leaving you to deal with the teacher's reminders or complaints.

Begrudging Parents

Another influential factor is *how your parents related to your financial dependence on them*. As a child, you were financially dependent on your parents for survival. If your parents begrudged you your material needs, that probably affected your beliefs about money. Your parents may have openly discussed the cost of raising you, or they may have actually withheld resources. For example, a parent might grumble about purchasing school supplies or even refuse to buy them. A mother who purchases toys for her child while reminding him that she never had any toys as a child instills guilt in the child. A father who complains about the cost of the child's needs and then purchases things for himself predisposes that child to splurge as an adult. Other types of dysfunctional behavior include broken promises of money, allowances, or gifts; never saying no or always saying no; or reprimanding children about their needs with statements such as "Didn't I tell you we don't have enough money?"

Particularly difficult are cases in which parents value material objects over their children's self-esteem. This type of parent scolds the child for spilling juice on the carpet by emphasizing the cost of the carpet. The child is left confused about whether they have any value beyond that of the material objects that surround them.

Later on, a begrudging parent refuses to pay for college because he or she either didn't attend or had to work through college. As elders, these same parents use guilt with references to future inheritance. They say things like, "You don't really deserve this inheritance because you didn't work for it like I did," or "When I'm gone, you're going to have a lot of money." In severe cases, parents threaten to take the inheritance away unless adult offspring abide by parental requests. In all these cases, the parent is unresolved about the child's dependence on them and actively manipulates the child through overindulgence or withholding. Even if money isn't exchanged, the parent's intentional reference to the child's financial dependence leaves the child confused.

Parental Conflicts about Money

Another factor is how your parents *related to each other about money.* Power struggles over finances are often at the heart of a financially dysfunctional family. Your parents may have engaged in general arguments about money or about their overall life circumstances. Your parents may have had constant conflicts over values and about what is deemed materially necessary for a good life. One of your parents may have been disappointed in the other's earning potential or spending habits. You may have witnessed one parent hide and sneak about issues related to money or push for purchases while the other parent resisted. Even when both partners contribute equally to the family's finances, different beliefs and behaviors lead to power struggles.

 POWER STRUGGLES OVER FINANCES ARE OFTEN AT THE HEART OF A FINANCIALLY DYSFUNCTIONAL FAMILY.

If your parents were unable to negotiate and share power effectively, you may have entered the boxing ring with them. For example, a father spends freely on his children for the latest toys, while the children witness their mother begging for money to fix the clothes dryer. Or perhaps the father won't say no to his wife's overspending, but enlists the children to do without necessities so the mother can continue her spending habits.

In some of these families, children learn to play the conflict to their advantage. They turn to the more lenient parent for desired items and instigate more parental conflict. This results in children who are torn between meeting their own needs and maintaining parental harmony.

In particularly problematic power struggles, the child continues to be brought into the middle of arguments even after the dissolution of a marriage. This is the type of situation in which a child is informed that a father can't afford to pay for college because of the child support he's had to pay the mother. The unresolved issues turn money into the vehicle to act out power in the relationship. But money is not the primary issue; power and control are.

Living with parents who have a tug-of-war with each other about money precludes children from learning money management and money negotiation skills. More important, *these arguments spotlight money not as a tool in life, but as an arena for conflict.* This sets the stage for financial hiding, secrecy, and problematic money behaviors later in life.

Innate and Learned Preferences

Parental attitudes and relationship to money, as we have seen, influence a child's behavior. If your parents were content with their financial life and lifestyle, they probably created a healthy climate for the home. On the other hand, if your parents were constantly dissatisfied with their financial situation, it's likely to have adversely affected you. *Every child unconsciously absorbs the parental attitudes.* This leads to confusion. For example, James remembers how much his mother and father wanted to get ahead in life. His mother, driven by feelings of inadequacy, worked furiously because she wanted the family to live in an upscale suburb. Even though his mother's income provided the same opportunities his friends had, James never felt he measured up. He had absorbed his mother's sense of inadequacy. As an adult, James rebelled against his parents' attitudes and became a financial underachiever. He always found himself in arguments with his bosses and was passed up for several promotions. He sought therapy when he was fired from his last job.

While parental behavior creates learned values and characteristics in a child, every child also has his or her own innate psychological temperament. The result: each and every person has different material desires and a different level of what constitutes material (or financial) satisfaction. Everyone has a unique satiety point—the point of "enoughness." Some folks want many pairs of shoes, while others are happy with one good pair. Some feel wasteful taking a ten-minute shower; others water their lawn daily. Some people want more opportunities to have excitement, so no matter how many times they go to hockey games, they want to have tickets to more games. Whatever one's temperament, a healthy relationship to money includes finding the point of enoughness. When there is no point of financial satisfaction, there's likely to be a problematic relationship to money.

How Outer Factors Influence Money Addiction

Beyond the factors in the home, two external factors—your birth generation (and its media) and your unexpected life circumstances—influence the creation of a money addiction.

Generation

The generation you are born into influences your money attitudes. For instance, if your cohort is Gen X (born in the years from 1965 to 1976) or Gen Y (born 1977 to 2000), you obviously have perspectives on money very different from those of people who grew up during the Great Depression in the United States. If you are a baby boomer (born 1946 to 1965), you are likely to have very different money attitudes from all three of those generations. Each generation lives through different historical and cultural events that influence values and worldview.

Different types of purchases are necessary in each period of history. Earlier generations focused on physical survival, and the bulk of a person's paycheck went toward necessities like housing, food, clothing, and medical care. More recent generations need to spend a percentage of their income on repaying student loan debt and keeping up with technological advances. In addition, different periods in history offer different social, governmental, and educational opportunities.

 ADVERTISING HAS CHANGED THROUGH THE GENERATIONS. MODERN-DAY ADVERTISING IS MUCH MORE POWERFUL THAN ADVERTISEMENTS OF THE PAST.

Advertising has changed through the generations. Modern-day advertising is much more powerful than advertisements of the past. As noted in chapter 1, modern advertisements promise spiritual and social rewards *through the purchase of products*. These ads offer solutions to problems that no material object could ever solve. If you grew up during the fifties and sixties, you witnessed advertisements that were designed merely to demonstrate the product and remind viewers of its availability. Advertisers have grown increasingly sophisticated since then. Contemporary ads employ highly effective and persuasive art and science to manipulate your desires and thought processes.

Modern-day ads don't promote concrete features and benefits of products; they infiltrate your psyche to teach you that *material things are necessary and deserved.* Modern ads teach us directly and subliminally that material products will meet inner emotional needs. Given the prevalence of media—especially the Internet and television—this amounts to continual brainwashing that drives us to seek material relief for nonmaterial woes.

This is most apparent for Gen X and Gen Y. If you were born after 1965, you've been raised with enormous media stimulation and have had your desires specifically targeted by a highly sophisticated media environment. You've been exposed to more advertising through more media outlets—print, broadcast, cable television, Internet, and cell phone advertising—than any other generation in history.

Unexpected Life Changes or Circumstances

There are many personal life experiences that influence beliefs and your relationship with money. You are sure to have your beliefs altered if you've been laid off after many years of service to a company, been transferred to another state, or been employed in an industry that becomes obsolete (or is outsourced to a country with lower wages). Your beliefs about money, dependence, and loyalty are apt to change if your employer downsizes or cuts pension plans in order to stay afloat. Major corporations, under the weight of collapse or corruption, take these actions regularly now. Technological advancement creates some new opportunities and careers, and shuts down others. Many other life experiences also intervene: having a boss who doesn't support employee advancement, who is abusive, or who is dishonest; marrying into a family with severe financial dysfunctions; establishing a business partnership with the wrong person; undergoing medical catastrophes or disasters such as fires; and on and on.

Of course, there are many life experiences that positively affect how you feel and act with money. Inspiring bosses who extend extra effort to enable a career move or mentors who take you as a newcomer under their wing in a company also shape your worldview about money. Something as simple as encouraging words from an accountant or lawyer can make all the difference in helping you handle your finances.

Unexpected life changes alter us permanently, particularly if lifestyle or basic security is threatened. When faced with sudden changes beyond our control, our ability to cope is challenged. Some seize these life changes as opportunities for transformation. Others with less resiliency tip in the direction of financially dysfunctional behavior, even the beginnings of addiction.

Summary

Because money is a daily requirement in life and necessary for survival, money problems are often born out of a wide range of childhood and adult circumstances. These complex influences range from childhood trauma to family experiences to large generational forces. Any and all of these can result in financially dysfunctional behavior, even full-blown addiction. If you understand the complex contributors, there's greater possibility of avoiding a money addiction or of getting help when you recognize one.

Now that you know the types of experiences that contribute to a troubled relationship with money, let's turn to the next chapter, which will explore specific types of money addictions.

. . .

Types of Money Problems

Money problems and money addiction are complex because money itself is complex. Remember, money isn't "real." It is a *symbol* of exchange for work produced. As a symbol, it functions in two very important ways.

First, money is a *means to material satisfaction*. As such, we often equate money with the material goods we need to feel satisfied. People with an unhealthy relationship to money and material goods tend to indulge themselves materially (think *Lifestyles of the Rich and Famous*) or to deprive themselves (think of Ebenezer Scrooge).

Second, money is a proxy for security and power over the long term—over a lifetime and even beyond, for those who will bequeath money to heirs. In this form, money is a *resource to be managed* and tended over time. People with money problems relate to this aspect of money by either avoiding it (think of the phrase "money is dirty") or being obsessed with it (think of the characters in the film *Wall Street*).

It's helpful to see relationships to money as traveling along two continua, like the up/down and left/right lines in a graph.

The first continuum (the up/down line) relates to materialism, with *indulgers* at one end and *deprivers* at the other end. I call this the *materialism continuum*. The second continuum (the left/right line) relates to financial management, with *avoiders* at one end and *obsessors* at the other. I call this the *finance continuum*.

The Materialism Continuum

Indulgers find happiness in material possessions and use them to impress others. If you're an indulger, your sense of self-worth is based on image and the approval of others. Many indulgers spend money to be perceived as better than others and to see themselves as better. As an indulger, you tend to spend lavishly on yourself, drive expensive cars, have the latest technology, and give elaborate gifts to other people.

For example, if you are a compulsive indulger, you might go to Macy's and see a diamond necklace and become convinced that you have to own it. You feel no sense of restraint. You do not hear an inner voice asking, "Do I need this? How will I pay for it? What about my other bills?"

In similar situations, the resolutions to curb spending fly out the door, and any memory of the pain caused by previous indulgences is forgotten. The indulger believes that the next purchase "will make life better for me this time. This is really the thing, just this one thing, now. I want that. *I need that.*" When faced with their substance of choice (material purchases), indulgers are unaware of the irrationality of their behavior. They see no choice. They become myopic.

INDULGERS FIND HAPPINESS IN MATERIAL POSSESSIONS AND USE THEM TO IMPRESS OTHERS. **DEPRIVERS** DERIVE SATISFACTION FROM DENYING THEMSELVES MATERIAL GOODS.

Deprivers, on the other hand, derive satisfaction from denying themselves material goods. They see themselves as thrifty, practical, and having few needs. If you are a depriver, you either avoid handling money because of inadequacy and shame, or you tend to be preoccupied with accumulating money because of fear. Either way, you tend to deprive yourself, and you like being perceived as beyond worldly needs.

As a depriver, you have a difficult time letting go of money even for basic expenses. You tend to wear worn clothing, drive dangerously old vehicles, and keep broken items in your home. If you do accrue bills, you won't pay them, for instance, allowing car insurance to lapse or not paying your medical bills. You'll avoid making home repairs in order to hold onto your money. You'll keep paychecks without cashing them for long periods of time. You resent having to give anything to anyone, including yourself. Even buying Kleenex, socks, and underwear is an imposition. Because of this deprivation, you cannot truly discern what is necessary in life and what is not necessary.

In the extreme, deprivers who avoid money end up needing others to support them financially. Extreme deprivers who obsess about finance and wealth may not have many material items, but they accumulate money. Maintaining and preserving that pile of money is all that matters. Any expense, even an ordinary bill, is a threat to that pile.

The Finance Continuum

Money problems and money addiction also span a *finance continuum*. People at one end of the spectrum obsess about money and financial matters, and at the other end are people who avoid money and financial matters. The *obsessors* expend a lot of time and energy on these matters. If you lean this way, you relate more to materialistic dimensions of life and derive satisfaction from acquisition and accumulation, especially as an expression of wealth.

In contrast, the *avoiders* are less likely to value money or concern themselves with it; in fact, they are afraid of wealth and tend to see money as dirty. If you are an avoider, you can't understand why everyone makes such a big deal about money, and you probably wish it would go away so you wouldn't have to deal with it.

The Money Problems Matrix

So we have people who indulge in or deprive themselves of material goods. And we have people who avoid money and financial matters or obsess about them. But in fact, everyone, healthy or addicted, has concerns in all these areas. To make sense of this, it's easiest to consider the indulger/depriver continuum and the avoider/obsessor continuum at the same time.

Chart 4-1 brings together the two spectrums of money behaviors: indulger versus depriver and obsessor versus avoider. I call this tool the Money Problems Matrix. With this tool, you can better understand the many expressions of money addiction. It will enable you to think about the psychological needs that drive your particular problematic relationship with money, as well as begin to see how you can help yourself. Later on in this book, we'll discuss how to use the chart on your journey toward balance and recovery.

CHART 4-1

The Money Problems Matrix

Indulgers

People who *indulge* in material things

Are indulgent with purchasing, but avoid money matters

Are indulgent and obsessed about wealth and money matters

Avoiders

People who *avoid* wealth and financial matters

Obsessors

People who *obsess* on financial matters

Avoid money and materialism and deprive themselves

Obsess on wealth and money matters, but deprive themselves

Deprivers

People who *deprive* themselves of material things

This chart gives you a framework for understanding the variety of subtypes within these four quadrants. However, to simplify the discussion, the remainder of this chapter separates money addictions according to the particular type of indulging or depriving. The names for these subtypes do a good job of describing what the behaviors look like. We'll explore these types in this chapter.

Indulgers who obsess on financial matters include:

• Compulsive spenders

• Compulsive shoppers

• Compulsive debtors

Indulgers who avoid financial matters include:

• Financial dependents

• Financial violators

Deprivers who obsess on financial matters include:

• Hoarders

Deprivers who avoid financial matters include:

• Financial underachievers

• Money averters

These categories are not exclusive. Money problems and money addictions manifest in myriad ways, even in the same individual. You can be a compulsive shopper when it comes to clothing, but hoard your money when it comes to spending on your home or education. You can also be a financial underachiever and be financially dependent. Or you can be a compulsive shopper, spender, and debtor.

In order to appropriately help yourself, you'll want to understand both the range of financial behaviors and how they overlap. As you might expect, indulgers are the easiest to spot and more likely to seek help. In contrast, deprivers are often hidden and—due to their preference for self-denial—much less likely to reach out for help. It is often close family and friends who identify deprivers.

Indulgers

As noted, indulgers express their money problems through behaviors that involve overspending on themselves or others. They most often appear as compulsive spenders, compulsive shoppers, compulsive debtors, financial dependents, or financial violators.

Compulsive Spenders

Compulsive spenders are the most common of the problem users and money addicts, and a model of the "indulger" form of the addiction. Like a child, a compulsive spender can't say no to spending money. If you are a compulsive spender, you're unrealistic about how far money will go. You may spend your tax refund, bonus, and even your paychecks two or three times over—often before you receive the money. When rent is due, you are shocked to find you don't have enough to pay it. These addicts get high from spending and feel powerful when picking up the tab for meals or giving expensive gifts.

Compulsive spenders justify purchases without considering how to pay for them. If a $2,000 sofa catches their eye, for instance, they buy it. Their sense of self rests on the freedom to spend. They can't tolerate being left out and often spend to excess in group situations. If you are a compulsive spender, you don't necessarily spend on material objects; you might overspend on services or experiences such as massage or travel. There's an insatiable feeling that you do not have enough, even with constant spending.

Some compulsive spenders don't indulge themselves, but compulsively spend on others. They can't say no to requests for purchases or loans. If you are this type of compulsive spender, you probably confuse money with love and believe that buying things for others is giving love. For example, while Pat and Elizabeth were on vacation in Mexico, Elizabeth fell in love with a $900 turquoise necklace. Even though Pat knew they couldn't afford it, he was unwilling to disappoint his wife and paid for the necklace with credit.

Other compulsive spenders spend excessively on children. If you are of this type, you'll ensure your children wear stylish clothing, even if you buy your own clothes on discount or secondhand. These spenders accumulate debt by laying out large sums of money for private school and college, travel, and vehicles for the children. This type of spender stays in denial for years, never informing the children of the hardship. In the extreme, this type of compulsive spender may end up supporting

TYPES OF INDULGERS

- **Compulsive Spenders**
  Compulsive spenders can't say no to spending money. They are unrealistic about how far money will go.

- **Compulsive Shoppers**
  Compulsive shoppers shop to alter moods and alleviate intolerable emotions, such as boredom, depression, or anxiety.

- **Compulsive Debtors**
  Compulsive debtors have a persistent need to be in debt. They also have additional debts, such as home equity loans, debts to family members, and medical providers.

- **Financial Dependents**
  Financial dependents are indulgers who avoid money matters. They remain under-employed and childlike regarding money and expect others to spend on them.

- **Financial Violators**
  Financial violators believe that rules about money should be different for them than for other people. They bend rules, violate boundaries, and break laws.

adult children even though it puts them into debt, justifying it as parental responsibility.

Compulsive spending on others is also common for women who overspend on friends or buy extravagant gifts for acquaintances, gifts that are not congruent with the level of intimacy in the relationship.

Compulsive Shoppers

Compulsive shoppers shop to alter moods and alleviate intolerable emotions, such as boredom, depression, or anxiety. If you're a compulsive shopper, you tend to shop as a way to fill inner voids and medicate yourself. Attentive shop clerks are perceived as friends who give you attention, thus helping you avoid painful feelings of loneliness. You may feel a rush or a high when in stores or malls. Afterward, you may not remember what you purchased; you may even purchase duplicate items without realizing it. If you're a compulsive shopper, you enjoy being up on trends and know exactly where to find items. Compulsive shoppers shop anywhere and everywhere—regular retail stores, antique malls, the Internet, mail-order catalogs, garage sales, and auction houses.

Like compulsive spenders, compulsive shoppers spend outlandish amounts and derive great pleasure from purchasing goods and services. However, they differ from compulsive spenders in that their primary focus is on *the thrill of shopping*—that is, the main feature of their behavior is shopping (often with a purchase), while the primary feature for compulsive spenders is any type of spending.

Although many compulsive shoppers are in debt, it is not uncommon for compulsive shoppers to be able to afford their buying habits, at least in the early stages of the addiction. However, as the disease progresses, the purchases eventually exceed the income.

There are five types of compulsive shoppers: the *bargain hunter,* the *image shopper,* the *shopping bulimic,* the *perfection shopper,* and the *collector shopper.* I am indebted to author Donna Boundy for the terms *bargain hunter, image shopper,* and *shopping bulimic.*[1]

BARGAIN HUNTERS

Bargain hunters derive thrills from finding cheap deals. If you are a bargain hunter, you'll purchase large quantities when you find an item on sale, even if you don't need it. The bargain hunter can also be obsessed or preoccupied with coupons, rebates, and frequent shopper clubs. For example, Lisa's mom gave her nine Christmas-themed sweaters, but Lisa can count on getting another one next year. Her mom can't resist buying them on clearance.

IMAGE SHOPPERS

Image shoppers purchase to impress others. If you shop for highly visible items and like to be seen in status automobiles, expensive jewelry, and designer clothing, you are probably an image shopper. Image shoppers don't like "average," and are particularly vulnerable to media promises of self-esteem through ownership. For example, Shelly recently purchased a top-of-the-line $50,000 SUV that left her household with a $1,100 monthly payment. Her husband was angry when they returned from the dealership because he would have been happy with a vehicle half the price. Shelly insisted upon the more expensive one, stating, "Everyone has the $25,000 model."

SHOPPING BULIMICS

Shopping bulimics are compulsive shoppers who experience remorse after their purchase and are driven to return items to alleviate guilt. If you are in this category, you believe you must have the item you see when you are shopping, but afterward, you crash into regret and shame and lose any pleasure in your purchase. To alleviate the painful aftereffect, you return the item. You then feel a sense of relief, believing you've saved money— even though you haven't, because you've simply returned an item. Often, this sense of relief and savings leads you to spend the same money again even before leaving the store.

PERFECTION SHOPPERS

Perfection shoppers pursue an ideal item to fulfill an imagined fantasy. If you are a perfection shopper, you seek to find the precise accessory for an outfit or the perfect home décor item. Shopping may involve visiting multiple stores in search of this idealized image. For example, when staying in a hotel in New York City, Amber fell in love with the cushions in the hotel lobby because they matched her living room. Upon her return, she decided she had to have the pillows and phoned the hotel and insisted the manager trace the source of the pillows so she could purchase them.

COLLECTOR SHOPPERS

Many people purchase items because they fit into a collection of some sort. Collector shoppers, however, are out of control and amass collections far beyond their ability to pay for them. Joseph began his gun and knife collection after inheriting two antique guns and a knife. Now he attends trade shows to add to his collection. He promises himself he just wants to see what's available, but he always comes home with new items, even though he can't make his rent.

Compulsive Debtors

Compulsive debtors are another type of indulger. They can be thought of as compulsive spenders who have ratcheted the disorder up a notch and have a persistent need to be in debt. While the compulsive spender has to spend the $20 in their pocket, the compulsive debtor is compelled to spend the $20 and more, just to feel the rush of living perpetually on the edge. If you are a compulsive debtor, you like the stimulation of financial juggling. As you continue this behavior, you grow increasingly tolerant of financial crises. Like compulsive spenders and shoppers, there's usually credit card debt, but compulsive debtors also have additional debts, such as home equity loans, debts to family members, medical providers, and utility companies.

Typical compulsive debtors are compulsive spenders who live beyond their means over many years. They usually increase spending as their income increases. For example, Jason earned $40,000 a year but was $12,000 in debt, well over what his income could tolerate. His steep monthly mortgage and large credit card payment left him unable to pay for any other large expense. Recently, he did not have the cash to pay for new brakes on his $30,000 car. So in one month, he charged the brakes and a $400 veterinary bill to his credit card. Then he got a great annual bonus and a raise—and promptly purchased a luxury car rather than paying down debt.

Compulsive debtors come in every income bracket. Frank makes $350,000 a year as a dentist, but is $78,000 in credit card debt. He has been in debt since high school. After he paid off his student loans, he joined a country club and bought a $60,000 Lexus. Then he began splurging on fine art. Frank is still unable to keep himself from financial chaos.

A compulsive debtor who also owns a business usually expands the debt into business spending as well. As with personal debt, the business debt becomes progressively worse over time. The problem debtor begins by starting or buying a business that does not succeed, and then borrows money to try to save it. Some even start additional businesses, hoping the second business will fund the first one. They borrow money for the business that they then can't repay, and the cycle progresses. Sometimes the business never makes enough money to make the payroll, but the addict/owner can't see the situation for what it is.

For example, Elise owns a small public relations firm. She began her compulsive debt problem two years after she ventured into her own business. A natural salesperson, Elise easily gains the trust of potential clients, and earning money has always come easily for her. Her business has a high income, enabling her to have a cutting-edge Web site, a BMW, and a full-time office assistant. The business has a $58,000 credit line debt, and personally she owes $26,000 on credit cards. Her total debt has been as high as $150,000, which took seven years to pay off. She's now in the same situation again. When there was a slight downturn for the business, she panicked and began to spend on advertising. She lives in constant fear of her business declining and stays perpetually in debt because of it.

Financial Dependents

Financial dependents are indulgers who avoid money matters. They remain underemployed and childlike regarding money and expect others to spend on them. If you are a financial dependent, you don't want to provide for yourself. Because of this, you will remain in an unhappy marriage merely for the financial support. You may not feel confident that you can earn a living, or you might feel you deserve to have someone else support you. Either way, you don't want any responsibility for finances. If your avoidance of money management contributes to financial hardship of your family, you are likely to get angry when your partner mentions the situation. For example, Maria married Luke because she knew that he came from a wealthy family and that he would one day inherit money, thereby setting herself up for financial security. Throughout the course of their marriage, she indulged herself in extravagant expenses, such as a personal assistant, clothing binges, and remodeling projects, taking no responsibility for the depletion of the family resources. When her husband complained, she told him that he wasn't making enough money.

In another example, Jennifer, recently divorced, is in search of a rich husband to support her despite her own six-figure income. Because she is also a compulsive debtor and lives in houses much beyond what she can afford, she has been evicted from three homes. She has her own money, but insists that others take care of her financially—either her former landlords or the men she is involved with.

Financial Violators

Financial violators believe that rules about money should be different for them than for other people. They bend rules, violate boundaries, and break laws. Financial violators must have the upper hand in every money interchange. These encroachments extend from simple violations, such as stealing office supplies or cheating on time cards, to embezzlement or fraud. For instance, Sharon uses a variety of tactics to get bargains, including bullying and outright dishonesty. She owns a business that handles a lot of cash and has several methods to launder a portion of this cash without paying taxes. When her adult son returned home to attend graduate school, she fudged the student loan application to ensure grant money. Sharon feels she deserves special privileges, and as is the case with addictions, her risky behaviors have grown worse. Such behaviors are typically not prosecuted as crimes even though some of them are outright illegal.

❖

All indulgers, except for financial violators, experience a common emotional cycle. This cycle involves participating in behaviors related to overspending and then feeling ashamed for having overspent, followed by repetitions of the cycle to alleviate the shame. This cycle is characteristic of other addictions (chemical, food, sex, and gambling) as well. Because addicts are truly powerless over the behavior, they cannot see what they are doing when they are doing it. But, after the buzz wears off, they have faint feelings of self-reproach. So, in an effort to obliterate these painful moments, addicts resume the behavior that makes them feel better.

Deprivers

As noted, deprivers express their money problems or money addiction through overcontrolled spending. They see themselves (and like to be seen) as thrifty, practical, and having few needs. They want other people to see them as not needing much. The deprivers who obsess about finances are called *hoarders;* the deprivers who avoid financial matters are termed *financial underachievers* and *money averters.*

Hoarders

Hoarders have a pathological fear of spending and letting go of money to such an extent that they jeopardize relationships, health, safety, and financial well-being. Because hoarders obsess about wealth, they often have significant financial resources. Even with money in the bank, they fear losing money and being taken advantage of by others. Most of all they fear their own needs and desires. They hoard their paycheck by not depositing it. They write out checks to pay bills, but don't mail them on time, not wanting to release the money. If you are a hoarder, you'll avoid going to the doctor or the dentist even when you are ill. You resent paying for services such as furnace repair or car maintenance, even when neglecting this upkeep is dangerous. In the extreme, hoarders drive long distances to save money on an item or to find a parking meter with money already on it.

For example, Derek accrued exorbitant costs for his roof repair because he refused to repair it when it first started leaking. Further, the insulation in his home became moldy, exposing him to serious health risks. Derek's case is a good example of the deep irony of hoarders: they fear taking risks, but often live more dangerously because of their frugality. The "logic" of saving money regardless of the cost or danger outweighs the more powerful logic that an ounce of prevention is worth a pound of cure.

To be sure, people need to hoard when living through a depression, war, or famine. But when hoarding is based on illogical fear rather than necessity, it is evidence of a money addiction. Hoarding is an addiction if it causes problems in a number of relationships. For instance, Sarah, a wealthy computer scientist with lots of money in the bank, will not let herself eat at a restaurant without a half-off coupon. Her friends resent this behavior; sometimes less successful friends have even offered to pay for her.

Another example is Rod, a successful physician. His lifelong buddy complained about him, "A bunch of us friends would go out to eat together, everyone would put in their order, and Rod would deliberate about his order. Finally, he'd choose something meager. Then when our food arrived, he'd look enviously at us enjoying our meals. He'd then scrounge the leftovers. Another time when we visited him for a long weekend, we all went to the grocery store so we could contribute. At the counter, Rod had a quarter of a watermelon in his hands, and fretted over the extra cost of the watermelon. He ultimately decided against it, and put it back. Here's our lifelong friend who can't enjoy the pleasure of sharing with us. I never thought money would come between us, but this last visit was so uncomfortable, I'm no longer interested in visiting him."

Another example of a hoarder is Lewis, who is fearful of losing his life savings. Lewis and his wife, Mary, began couples therapy because they wanted to learn communication skills. After four months of successful therapy, Lewis warned Mary that he would divorce her if her spending ever caused them to go below a certain amount in the bank. The marriage counselor supported Lewis in this decision, until Mary exposed the extent of the family wealth, a $3 million inheritance in the bank. Mary also added that a few million more were likely on the way when his father passed away. Nevertheless, Lewis revealed that he would rather lose his marriage (a substantial emotional and financial cost) than tolerate a depletion of his stash—a clear example of the strange "logic" of hoarding.

Financial Underachievers

Financial underachievers express money problems and money addiction through an irrational, unconscious choice to avoid earning enough money to meet basic living expenses or earn below their skill or education level. If you are a financial underachiever, your money avoidance keeps you in an underpaying job for years, seemingly paralyzed and afraid to ask for raises or pursue advancement. Financial underachievers believe they are less attached to money and materialism and gain a sense of superiority because of the detachment. Financial underachievers report being immobilized and feel incompetent or unsuccessful in earning a living. As the disease progresses, these people eventually grow angry at others who are able to take risks and get ahead.

Evan has a graduate degree in business. During his college years he worked at a bakery. After graduation he stayed at the bakery. Now, ten years after graduating, he is still working at the bakery. He's been offered jobs to use his MBA and has turned them down. He's not satisfied at the bakery in the least, but he won't make a change. His addiction shows up in his compulsive underachievement.

Betty is a business consultant who charges $85 per hour for her services. Her national competitors charge $150 to $200 per hour. She does not charge for phone time and allows her clients to phone with questions instead of setting up actual meeting times. Some of these same clients have also begun to invite her to social events so they can pick her brain free of charge. Betty recognizes that she has a problem but is still fearful of raising her rates because she fears losing these clients. When she entered therapy, she was angry at her customers and her competitors. Her anger then spread to herself because she knew she was more experienced than her competitors, yet they charged higher fees. She was also angry at herself because she had begun to accrue a balance on her credit card that she couldn't pay. Once in therapy, she realized she had never earned as much as her peers, even though she considered herself equally talented.

Money Averters

Money averters are the flip side of financial violators. Financial violators violate other people's financial boundaries, while money averters allow others to take advantage of them financially. If you are a money averter, you don't believe you deserve money, and you won't pursue money owed to you. This behavior is common with service professionals who allow clients to accrue large balances and don't collect the outstanding invoices. For example Mike, a therapist in his sixties, faithfully sent a bill every month to his clients but never followed up to collect the money or held clients accountable if they didn't pay. He never discussed money owed to him in therapy sessions and continued to provide services to nonpayers despite the fact that he himself had no retirement savings of his own.

Jason spent twenty years building a business and sold part of it to someone who did not make the payments. He never followed up with legal recourse nor did he repossess the business; the buyer basically got the business for free.

Another example of this expression of money problems and money addiction includes people who don't return unneeded but new items, won't follow up with filing health insurance claims or tax refunds, or won't ask for repayment of personal loans. A money averter could also be thought of as a person who debts to himself or herself. Such a person has earned money and yet won't claim it. This person is conflicted about the role of money and fears potential confrontation or conflict with others surrounding the financial exchange.

Let's look at how all these types of problem users fit in the Money Problems Matrix, shown in chart 4-2.

CHART 4-2

Where Problem Users Fit in the Money Problems Matrix

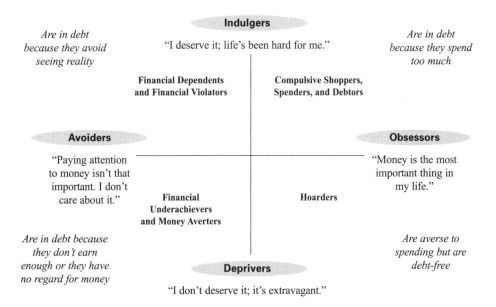

This chart shows the full spectrum of problem user and addictive money behaviors. You can see how all the types fit in relationship to (a) how they relate to material goods (they *indulge* themselves or *deprive* themselves) and (b) how they behave relative to financial matters (they *avoid* them or *obsess* over them). You can also see that *debt* is the primary symptom for three of the four main categories, while people in the fourth category avoid any form of spending.

Combinations of Behaviors

A person may have a combination of indulging and depriving behaviors. For example, Bill is a compulsive debtor and a hoarder. Despite reassurance from his financial adviser that he has already saved enough money to retire in comfort, he continues to save the maximum in his profit-sharing plan. He frequently checks his bank balance online to assure himself of how much money he has. He gets anxious if the number diminishes, and if it does he withholds payments on bills. The result is that despite having a small fortune for retirement, he is often late with mortgage and utility payments. At the same time, Bill likes to indulge in toys and trips. When Bill began his new astronomy hobby, he bought a new telescope. He charged a $4,000 trip to Bulgaria (to witness the solar eclipse) on his credit card. Because Bill puts so much of his money in savings, he cannot pay for these extravagances without using credit cards— and he consistently pays those late, accumulating excessive fees that keep him on the edge. Bill hoards money for retirement while he incurs debt.

A person can have two types of indulger behaviors, such as when the compulsive spending grows into a compulsive debt lifestyle. In this case, the indulger soothes himself through compulsive spending, which escalates into the thrill of living on the edge of debt.

Or a person can have two overlapping depriver tendencies. For example, Jill is a financial underachiever as well as a hoarder. Jill received a B.A. in English and now works three minimum-wage jobs, none of which uses her exemplary writing talents. She needs better, sturdier shoes for the long hours she spends waiting tables, yet she doesn't allow herself to spend money on them. Her old car constantly needs repair, but she can't afford to buy a new one, and she won't go to the movies or out to dinner with friends.

Chart 4-3 provides a thumbnail description of each subtype.

Summary

Most people have periods in their lives when money management is troublesome. Healthy saving and spending habits take time to develop. However, you have a problem when your money problems have become compulsive and progressive.

Problematic money users and full-blown addicts fall somewhere along two continua of the Money Problems Matrix. One continuum illustrates a person's

CHART 4-3

Summary of Money-Related Addictions

Indulgers	
Compulsive Spenders	Cannot keep money—if it's there, it's spent on anything and anybody. Don't necessarily like to shop. Can spend excessively on others and can't say no to others' requests.
Compulsive Shoppers	Shop to self-medicate. Like the thrill of shopping and following popular trends in pursuit of the "right" item. Types include bargain hunters, image shoppers, shopping bulimics, perfection shoppers, and collector shoppers.
Compulsive Debtors	Develop chronic indebtedness. Borrowing money extends beyond financial institutions to family and friends. Some own small businesses.
Financial Dependents	Expect others to spend on them and take care of them financially.
Financial Violators	Break financial boundaries. Take what is not theirs.
Deprivers	
Hoarders	Like to accumulate money. Fear spending money.
Financial Underachievers	Despite having the capability to do so, don't earn enough to meet basic expenses or don't earn up to their skill or education level.
Money Averters	Exhibit financial passivity. Won't pursue money that is due them.

relationship to material goods; at one end of the continuum are people who *indulge* in material goods, and at the other end are people who *deprive* themselves of material goods. The second continuum, finance, highlights how a person relates to financial matters; at one pole are people with the tendency to obsess about money and financial matters, and at the other end are people who avoid money and financial matters. As you review the types of money behaviors, you can look for those behaviors in yourself. Think about whether and when you tend to indulge in material goods or deprive yourself of them. And think about whether you prefer to avoid all things related to the management of money or to obsess over it. Lastly, think about where you fit on the Money Problems Matrix.

Money problems and money addiction also influence partnerships, which we will discuss in the next chapter.

• • •

How Money Problems
Affect Relationships

So far, we've been concerned primarily with the impact the problem user or money addict has on him- or herself. But a hallmark of any addiction is its harmful consequences to other people. When money is at the heart of the addiction, the toll is great. In this chapter, we'll look at various ways that money addiction affects your relationships. But before we do that, let's look at how money works in a nonaddicted, if imperfect, couple relationship.

During Bonnie and Maurice's fifteen-year marriage, they have had many problems. These consist of communication difficulties; a troubled, mostly nonexistent sexual relationship; and major discrepancies in needs for social outlets. Their life is no Norman Rockwell painting, but they have managed to find much happiness in each other, their children, and their separate and mutual goals. They've accomplished many financial goals successfully and without strain, supporting each other to achieve material and lifestyle dreams. Bonnie longed to live on a lake, and though this wasn't his goal, Maurice agreed to the additional expense and work of a lake home, and has learned with time that being closer to nature comforts him. He decided to return to school to seek a graduate degree, and she was willing to work unusual hours and juggle child care to support his career change. He views her sometimes indulgent shopping for crafts as a charming part of her personality. She doesn't care about his interest in antique lanterns, but is glad that it makes him happy and accompanies him to auctions and flea markets, and she's happy to see their oldest daughter helping her father restore them. The successful navigation of finances as a means of achieving goals is a major positive feature of their relationship. Beyond that, it's a building block for their marriage: success in this arena gives both of these partners hope that they can resolve other marital difficulties as they continue to work on the marriage.

Healthy couples work together to achieve financial goals. Partners communicate about money in order to resolve conflicts and adjust to inherent differences in values, needs, interests, and desires. Both parties are capable of adjusting their own behavior and are willing to compromise. There isn't always perfect financial harmony, but there is enough trust to flex and flow with changes and new opportunities. Normal upswings and downswings in finances occur without anyone feeling unfairly deprived. In these partnerships, each person supports the other with risk-taking and career changes.

HEALTHY COUPLES WORK TOGETHER TO ACHIEVE FINANCIAL GOALS. PARTNERS COMMUNICATE ABOUT MONEY IN ORDER TO RESOLVE CONFLICTS AND ADJUST TO INHERENT DIFFERENCES IN VALUES, INTERESTS, AND DESIRES.

The healthy, rational sharing of financial well-being is truly an accomplishment. And here's why: when money is exchanged or shared between any two people, both become financially vulnerable and dependent. When you are in a relationship with another person, you need your partner to be fair, honest, and trustworthy in holding up the other end of the financial interdependence. You need to trust that your partner won't hurt you or take advantage of you. You are also *emotionally* vulnerable and dependent in long-term relationships. You and your partner need each other to provide safety and security, so you can trust each other and build intimacy. Emotional intimacy requires trust that your partner won't abuse you or violate your boundaries. With this degree of dependence on one person, primitive feelings from childhood arise and often result in a more complicated financial partnership.

In chapter 3, "The Emotional Sources of Money Problems," we saw how your life story shapes your beliefs, feelings, and behaviors about money and finances. Both people bring their unique histories about money and security into the couple relationship, and their backgrounds affect their financial decisions and dealings. Childhood blueprints tend to collide, especially around early experiences of security and power. Let's explore how and why trouble spots arise.

Money in Relationships: The Inevitable Struggle

Many relationships don't have the financial ease that Bonnie and Maurice experienced. In fact, it's more typical to have disagreements about money. These clashes don't necessarily indicate problematic money use or even a money addiction. You and your partner bring not only childhood money beliefs and experiences, but also established adult patterns of spending and saving to the relationship. So it's common for couples to argue about how to spend money. In light of the myriad societal and familial contributors, it isn't alarming if there's conflict when two parties merge as a financial unit. This is a normal reaction when two individuals come together. Some couples argue simply because they don't communicate or lack skills to reconcile the different money styles. These factors bring about financial power struggles, but they do not automatically indicate money addiction.

However, for some, money is actually the principal arena of marital conflict. As we discovered in chapter 3, many areas of life having to do with security, power, and identity are revealed through money. Because money is basic to survival, it's basic to your sense of psychological and emotional security. For example, if you experienced trauma, financial insecurity, emotional turmoil, or financial dysfunction, it's likely that you have your own internal conflicts about money. You may not be aware of your own inner conflict. Your unconscious conflict directs your behaviors, and those behaviors strongly affect your partner. It's likely your partner also has unconscious conflicts about money. So when two people get together without consciousness of their own conflicts, the result is an unconscious struggle centering on money.

Couples frequently take polar opposite stances toward money, and this further complicates the struggle. These polarities occur when:

- One partner worries about money, and the other avoids thinking about it
- One partner focuses on earning and saving money, while the other focuses on spending money
- One partner values spending on pleasure and decorating, while the other values spending on practical needs such as roof or sewer repair
- One partner behaves like a parent, controlling the checkbook, while the other acts helpless and irresponsible

These polarities can undermine a relationship or enhance it. The opposing attitudes sometimes work against each other. For instance, the wife thinks the thrifty husband is trying to control her, and the husband thinks the spendthrift wife is trying to sabotage him. However, these same polarities can enhance a relationship and serve to bring balance. In such a situation, the husband benefits from the wife's spending, just as she benefits from his concerns for the budget. This couple may argue about money, but neither is an addict.

However, serious and long-standing financial conflict in a marriage can trigger a predisposed person to slip into full-blown addiction. The partner with an already troubled relationship to money might increasingly utilize dysfunctional money behaviors in an attempt to cope with marital tension.

Problem Users and Their Partners

In a relationship where there's problematic money use or money addiction, money conflicts dominate the interactions. These relationships involve deception and lies about spending, income, assets, and credit cards. Even when forced to disclose financial information, addicts always keep one or two secrets.

If you are the problem user or money addict in the relationship, your partner may not initially recognize your money addiction. He or she accepts whatever you say. Gradually, because all addictions grow worse over time, your partner recognizes there's a serious problem. However, your partner may not understand that you are out of control and can't stop your addiction.

Typically, your partner vacillates between anger and attempts to control you on the one hand, and apathy and denial with a sense of defeat on the other. The control can manifest through the following actions:

• Nagging and preaching
• Hiding credit cards
• Controlling bank accounts or the checkbook
• Paying your debts
• Restricting your life choices

When such partners discover that control and fixing don't work, they may collapse in defeat. They may appear as though they believe your lies, but really they are resigned to your dysfunctional use of money. It begins as quiet withdrawal from discussing finances. Outwardly, they could even support the continuation of the troubled behaviors, but meanwhile, they are disengaging from contact with you. They withhold financial information from you, and sometimes open separate or secret bank accounts. They pull away from socializing with you, may throw themselves into work or other activities, develop outside friendships, or begin romantic affairs. *Your partner has found a way to cope with your troubled relationship with money.* Marriages of this type can remain entrenched in this pattern for many years.

 IN A RELATIONSHIP WHERE THERE'S PROBLEMATIC MONEY USE OR MONEY ADDICTION, MONEY CONFLICTS DOMINATE THE INTERACTIONS.

The seeds to these dysfunctional financial patterns sometimes are sown prior to a formal commitment or marriage. At the outset of the relationship, you probably concealed how irresponsible your money behaviors previously were. Of course, you disclosed some information, but if you were a full-blown addict at the outset, you withheld the existence of one or two secrets. For example, you probably claimed to have paid off your debts, but later your partner found out the truth—that you only paid off half the balance, or only three out of the four cards were cut up.

This wasn't intentional deceit. In the beginning of your relationship, you probably viewed the marriage or partnership as a fresh start or opportunity to end your prior behaviors. Early on, when you were infatuated, you hoped the disclosure cleaned the slate. In denial, you believed that you could stop yourself and that the relationship was going to help you be better with money.

Your partner probably saw glimpses of the problem early on but didn't understand the extent or was too willing to overlook odd behaviors. Your partner denied his or her own perception, truly believing it couldn't be "that bad." Infatuated, your partner wanted to trust and believe your promises to change. Like you, he or she hoped it was all in the past.

In situations like this, the stage is set early in a relationship for the partner and the addict to collude in their denial of the extent of the problem. Neither partner sees the addiction for what it is. Both partners justify, rationalize, and minimize how it ultimately impacts the relationship. Both partners set themselves up for financial betrayal.

How Types of Money Problems Affect a Relationship

As you'll recall, money addicts come in two basic flavors, indulgers and deprivers, with a variety of expressions of each and tendencies to either avoid or obsess about financial matters. As you might expect, each has a unique impact on the partner or spouse, though all have serious consequences on interpersonal trust and on the financial health of the entire family. Below are some of the specific effects each behavior has on the family.

Indulgers

Indulgers come in many variations: compulsive spenders, compulsive shoppers, compulsive debtors, financial dependents, and financial violators. Each has characteristic impacts on a partner.

Compulsive spenders consume more than their share of the financial resources of the family. Whether they earn the money or not, their spending depletes it for everyone. Life opportunities become restricted for all involved, and basic needs are often unmet. Partners and family members grow resentful and, as the addiction progresses, embarrassed. This addiction causes family conflict and destroys family relationships. It is difficult to trust compulsive spenders because they lie. They cannot be relied on to be realistic about finances. Compulsive spending eventually results in financial ruin for entire families.

Compulsive shoppers generate resentment. Shopping takes time away from the family; the partner and children grow to resent it. The shopper spends countless hours in stores, on Internet sites, or browsing catalogs. The shopper's primary relationship is with the purchase, and he or she shows more concern for material possessions than for people. The "stuff" he or she buys takes up a lot of room in the house and displaces living space, and this restricts visitors because family members are embarrassed. While shopping, this person has tangled relationships with salespeople, all the while neglecting the child in tow. For shopping bulimics, the subsequent trips to the store (to return items and buy more) take even more time away from the family.

Compulsive debtors also seriously strain the family finances. The need to be in debt sometimes forces other family members to deny themselves necessities. The compulsive debtor may enlist the spouse, children, or other family members to borrow money for their spending habits. There are often major life changes; home foreclosure is common, and children are moved from school district to school district. In the extreme, the family ends up in a homeless shelter. There are dire legal consequences for the partner and family.

Financial dependents typically manipulate their spouses or partners to take care of them, and they may shame their partners for not making enough money. Partners codependently try to make their spouses happy and ultimately fail. Partners end up angry, passive-aggressive, and with low self-esteem. Financial dependents don't teach their children appropriate financial self-empowerment.

Financial violators don't respect financial boundaries, and because of this they cause embarrassment to loved ones. Family members become confused and humiliated if they witness violators aggressively pursuing other people's money. However, sometimes their transgressions are hidden from family; violators secretly steal from a child's piggy bank, birthday gifts, or college fund. Partners may be coerced into hiding illegal activities.

Deprivers

Deprivers come in fewer flavors than indulgers, but their impact can be just as confusing and devastating. They include hoarders, financial underachievers, and money averters.

Hoarders keep total control of their partners' spending and eventually expect everyone involved to be deprived also. Because their primary relationship is with an abstract object—money in the bank—rather than with people, interpersonal relationships are severely impaired. Family members become embittered when they witness addicts depriving themselves and subsequently depriving everyone else. Family members are forbidden to touch or enjoy the sometimes massive accumulations of money. This causes conflicts in the family. Partners and children are deprived of living freely, without financial fears, and children grow up with distortions about finances.

Financial underachievers deprive their partners and families of financial security and put pressure on their partners to provide for them. The financial underachiever avoids money matters, and this can be expressed as not wanting to "keep up with the Joneses," even when the partner's goal is not status but simply having enough to feel comfortable. The financial underachiever perceives the partner to be extravagant and materialistic, and constantly vetoes suggestions for personal improvement, becoming angry if the partner wants more. He or she deprives family members of financial normalcy, leaving off-spring confused about earning a living. As they mature, children of financial underachievers may become too focused on financial success or may tend to avoid it. Sometimes, children pity the parent.

Money averters put family in financial jeopardy because they do not pursue the money that is due them. Other family members must step up to the plate to take action. Because the money averter declines ownership of his or her money or property, the spouse and children feel angry as others get the money that is rightly theirs. The family is also angry when the addict passively resists the needs of the family.

When Partners Are Codependents

Many partners of people with money problems are codependent. When money problems exist in a relationship, a *codependent* derives self-esteem by controlling the emotions and financial behaviors of the problem money user. Codependents appear to put their own needs aside in order to take care of the problem user. Codependents are "addicted" to control of their partner. Because codependents believe they are in control of the problem, they buffer the problem money user from personal responsibility for the couple's financial difficulties. This way, neither faces the seriousness of the problem. In an extreme case, the codependent partner further jeopardizes his or her own finances by cosigning for additional loans or borrowing money to help the problem user.

Codependents cater to, support, or unconsciously encourage their partner's disordered behavior, though they would never admit to it. They make excuses and rationalize the partner's extreme financial needs. The codependent "over-looks" the new clothes in the closet or the flat screen TV. In fact, they gain self-esteem through these new items.

Sometimes codependents recognize that there is a problem, but they take on the rescuer or savior role to keep control and preserve their own image as the "good" partner. These rescuers get second jobs or pay off bills and debts, even if they have to borrow to do it.

Codependents are afraid their partners will become angry or threaten to leave, so they avoid honest discussion. Some codependents even have a "Go spend; I'll take care of everything" attitude, which furthers the dysfunction. One can easily see this in the example that follows of a codependent husband and compulsive spender wife.

Linda and Terry have been married for twenty-six years. In therapy, Terry reported that from the beginning of their courtship, he wanted to rescue Linda from her critical mother. Linda stayed home raising their two sons, and Terry traveled internationally as a salesman selling robots to factories. Linda began working part-time when the boys turned fourteen and sixteen. At first, Terry's income easily allowed her to dabble in antique collecting. Linda began to shop for her friends and started to sell at flea markets. Her "hobby" escalated through the years to $57,000 on credit cards. Terry noticed the credit card bill climbing, so he remained on the road longer to make more money. He liked providing for the family and had no intention of making any changes. However, deteriorating health due to complications from surgery left him unable to fly. The seriousness of his health condition woke him up to the financial reality of his marriage, and he grew angry about the debt. Ironically, the couple entered therapy because of Terry's anger, not Linda's compulsive spending.

 CODEPENDENTS CATER TO, SUPPORT, OR UNCONSCIOUSLY ENCOURAGE THEIR PARTNER'S DISORDERED BEHAVIOR, THOUGH THEY WOULD NEVER ADMIT TO IT.

Codependents will go to great lengths to enable a problem user or money addict, as the following example illustrates. Ed and his thirty-year-old daughter, Heather, have been locked in a vicious cycle for her entire adult life. She gets into trouble financially; he rescues her. Ed manages most of Heather's financial affairs: he balances her checkbook, writes the checks for her bills, and helps her complete job applications. Despite this caretaking pattern, Ed berates Heather for her irresponsible behavior each time she gets into trouble, thus reinforcing her belief that she is incompetent and unable to handle things on her own. Heather has a history of chasing after unrealistic jobs and has been unable to hold down a steady, secure job for any length of time. Most recently her daydreams took her to Florida in search of a modeling job. Ed didn't hear from her for six months, but was able to trace her movements by the activity on his Visa statements, since her card was under his name. Heather ran up $6,000 on the credit cards, staying in hotels and eating out. When she finally came home, Ed confronted her about her reckless spending. Heather insisted that she had been looking for work and didn't want to come home until she found something, but she had been unsuccessful. Playing on her latest, expensive failure, Ed suggested she take a job as a receptionist at his friend Gerry's office. Ed then paid the Visa bill.

Soon after, Heather had a car accident, her third. Ed was furious when he found out that she had canceled the car insurance, but Heather claimed she was trying to be responsible and save money. Her car was a wreck, she didn't have a job, and she couldn't afford to pay the fine for not having insurance. Ed spent hours on the phone tracking down another used car and getting her insurance reinstated, but was livid when Heather refused to accept a used car. She insisted on a new one, saying that she needed to look the part when interviewing for high-profile modeling jobs. Ed refused to buy a new car, but he didn't stop his codependent enabling. He drove Heather to her interviews and wherever else she needed to go.

These scenarios are not uncommon. It is typical of problem money users and money addicts to mismanage money over a period of years while the codependent remains in denial. When a spouse suddenly discovers what a partner has done, the sense of betrayal is deep. This betrayal can result in major economic consequences for the codependent partner when he or she is legally responsible to pay the debts.

Appendix A, "Are You Codependent?" (page 181), includes a set of questions to help you explore whether you may be codependent.

When Two Problem Users Are Involved

Often money problems occur on *both* sides of the relationship. In such a relationship, the addictive money behaviors collide, compete, or collude with each other. Moreover, two denial systems are at work. Some of the more common combinations include:

- Hoarder and compulsive spender
- Two compulsive spenders
- Financial underachiever and financial dependent
- Two financial underachievers

Hoarder and Compulsive Spender

The most common type of pairing is the hoarder and the compulsive spender. In this case, each attempts to control the spending behavior of the other. They push and pull against each other, vying for control to balance the situation.

Hoarders thrive on deprivation. They gain reward by prohibiting themselves from needed purchases. They may also restrict, or attempt to restrict, their partners' purchases, fearing a lack of money in the bank. In response, compulsive spenders overspend in an effort to "balance" the perceived extreme hoarding and deprivation and to prove to their partners that they cannot be controlled or withheld from.

 HOARDERS THRIVE ON DEPRIVATION. IN RESPONSE, COMPULSIVE SPENDERS OVERSPEND IN AN EFFORT TO "BALANCE" THE PERCEIVED EXTREME HOARDING AND DEPRIVATION.

This is the most common marital pattern with regard to money. There is a collusion of disorders—one partner seeks esteem or power through possession of objects and material image, and the other seeks comfort or power through deprivation and accumulation of money. One makes a mess, and the other cleans it up by taking charge of the checkbook or putting the problem spender on a budget. One controls, one retaliates; neither speaks about the dance. *Each feels superior to the other.* The spender believes he has superior taste or knows how to have fun. The hoarder believes she is superior because she can clean up the financial mess, she is sensible, and without her the spender would be penniless.

In couples, this looks very much like a parent/child relationship. For example, a hoarder husband may not allow his wife to buy niceties for herself, so in retaliation, whether conscious or unconscious, she overspends on something like groceries, purchasing only gourmet prepared foods. Or a compulsive spending husband, whenever he has extra money in the bank, may go out and treat himself to up-to-date electronics. The hoarding wife, in compensation, may insist that whenever there is extra money, they apply it toward their mortgage balance. The wife in this case is willing to do without items for herself to see that the mortgage gets paid down faster.

Two Compulsive Spenders

When two compulsive spenders have a relationship, both are in denial and they collude in their shared problem. They both overcharge their credit cards, and neither makes a plan or a budget. Both live in the moment, avoiding conflict and appearing to be a happy, carefree couple. They share an unspoken agreement that neither will challenge the other about spending.

For example, Lloyd and Jane have been in debt their entire marriage. Lloyd works as a computer programmer, and Jane is a stay-at-home mom for their four-year-old daughter. From the outside, it's difficult to see that they are compulsive spenders. Jane is very thrifty and buys her clothing from secondhand stores, even altering things that don't fit. Lloyd drives a midsize car and works as much overtime as he can get. But Jane got the idea for a new energy-efficient furnace, which they charged on their credit card. Then they decided new windows would contribute to the house's overall heat efficiency, and they charged those. To pay off those credit cards, they remortgaged and took a trip with the leftover money from the refinance. Then the basement began to leak, and the waterproofing job cost $9,000, which they charged. Even with all the debt, Jane is considering having the living room painted, though she worries that they have no retirement savings and no college savings for their daughter. They made all these purchases without forethought or planning.

Sometimes two compulsive spenders consciously or unconsciously compete to "one-up" each other when it comes to spending. If a husband buys a new car, the wife may feel justified in spending a lot of money on clothes to get her "fair share." She believes if she doesn't spend all the money she wants to, he will spend it before she has a chance to get what she wants. This type of relationship may go on for many years without either partner challenging the other's spending habits, all the while accruing joint debt.

Financial Underachiever and Financial Dependent

Sometimes a financial underachiever, who doesn't earn enough money to take care of basic needs, partners with a financial dependent who expects to be taken care of. The underachiever may get a second or third job to make sure they are able to afford nice things; all the while the partner isn't happy. The financial dependent blames the underachiever for not earning enough money for the desired lifestyle.

Two Financial Underachievers

Sometimes two financial underachievers will seek to stay impoverished. Both fear success and collude not to threaten the other. No one rocks the boat. One may never gain employment. For example, Andrea and Wilson have been together for nine years. When they married, Wilson was paying off debt from his previous marriage, and Andrea worked at the corner drugstore as a clerk. She also had a small settlement from her divorce. Wilson worked in his family's travel agency and was paid a basic salary plus commissions. The commissions declined when travel sales switched to the Internet. Because his mother owned the business, he felt he would someday inherit it and eventually make more money, so he never worried about saving to buy a home. Andrea broke her foot and wasn't able to work for nine months. She lost her small paycheck and never regained employment because her broken foot continued to cause problems. In their mid-fifties, neither of them knew how much it cost them monthly to live, nor had they ever earned enough money to live without credit cards. Both secretly expected the other to provide the money.

Problem Users Involved with Healthy Money Managers

This chapter opened with a picture of healthy money management in a normal marriage. Money addicts *can* be involved with healthy money managers, and if you are involved with a money addict, you can learn to manage healthily in the situation, just as a partner can learn to live serenely with an alcoholic. When an addict is involved in a relationship with a healthy money manager, troublesome behavior will be confronted and challenged in such a way that the money addict is held accountable for his or her behavior. Healthy, noncodependent people clearly know when something is wrong and do not question whether or not they themselves are a part of the problem. There is no second-guessing, self-scrutiny, or attempt to rescue the addict with financial solutions. Quite often healthy people will insist that the addict get help. They may threaten to terminate the relationship if the addict does not comply. In addition, healthy people know how to take care of themselves financially and do not set themselves up to be used or abused by the money addict's destructive behavior; they will even take legal action (having names removed from accounts or separating bank accounts, for example) to protect themselves if necessary.

George and Harold had been partners for many years. As much as George cared for Harold, he was well aware of Harold's irresponsibility when handling his own finances, which had gotten him into hot water more than once. George had taken it all in stride until one day when Harold asked him for a loan. George struggled with this request but finally agreed on one condition: he made Harold secure the loan by taking out a life insurance policy naming George as the beneficiary.

Other examples of self-protection include taking collateral for a loan, changing legal documents to disentangle financially, conducting a therapeutic intervention, going over the numbers with a money addict and demanding accountability for finances and debts, or calling upon the services of an accountant, financial planner, debt counselor, or therapist. In the end, the healthy partner may decide to leave the relationship.

Summary

Inevitably, money problems and money addiction spill over into the lives of significant others. The degree of intimacy and financial/legal commitment in a relationship influences the degree of hurt or damage that the person with money problems will inflict. Sometimes, problem users or addicts are intimately connected to codependents, and sometimes addicts find other addicts to partner with. In still other cases, the problem user gets involved with a person who knows how to take steps to maintain mental and financial well-being. Regardless of the situation, it is certain that a person with money problems will have a lasting effect on those around him or her.

The next chapter opens the second part of the book. We'll look at how people with money problems can help themselves, and offer hope for your loved one with a problem.

· · ·

PART
2

Solutions:
Untangling Yourself

Your Personal Money Behaviors

You may have breezed through the previous chapters. Please allow a bit more time for this chapter. You'll need a notebook and pen and some quiet time to think. Or, instead of a notebook, you may download and print out a free reproducible journal that contains the questions and worksheets in this book. Go to hazelden.org/bookstore; on the *Spent* page, click on "reproducible journal with worksheets." In fact, this chapter can only be fully written *by you*. This is the time and place for you to begin to look at your own behaviors around money and at how those behaviors developed over time.

In the first part of this chapter, you will find questions that explore the history of your behaviors with money. These questions explore your early experiences and the attitudes you learned about money in your family of origin. In the second part, you will find help to understand the discoveries you made while answering the questions.

The assessment questions that follow are divided into sections on your current financial behaviors and your financial history.

Pen and notebook ready? Good, let's begin!

Your Current Financial Behaviors

A book can't diagnose you, and it's not a good idea to diagnose yourself. But you can get a good start on understanding if you have a problem by answering the questions below. The answers to these eight questions start you on your way to exploring whether you have a money addiction.

1. Are you unable to stop spending money even when you know it causes problems? Describe.

2. Do you panic when you have to spend money? Describe.

3. Has your avoidance of financial responsibilities caused problems for you? Describe.

4. Is it difficult for you to earn enough money to support yourself? Describe.

5. Do you sometimes feel that you can't control yourself with money? For example, do you make promises to yourself about spending that you can't keep? Describe.

6. Do you conceal your behavior? Describe.

7. Has your problem worsened over time? Describe.

8. Has your problem affected others in your life? Describe.

If you answered yes to any of these basic questions, it's likely that you have a problematic, possibly even addictive relationship with money. The following questions will help you pinpoint your specific problematic behaviors.

Your Indulging and Depriving Behaviors

SPENDING HABITS (COMPULSIVE SPENDERS, SHOPPERS, AND DEBTORS)

1. Are you unable to keep cash in your wallet?

2. Are you anxious about whether you can pay your bills?

3. Do you have credit card debt? How much? Has it grown larger over time? Do you know where it came from?

4. Do you avoid opening the mail or hide it from others because of the bills you anticipate?

5. Do you hide purchases or take the price tags off items so family members will not know they are recent purchases?

6. Do you bounce checks regularly?

7. Are you unable to save money for large-ticket items like down payments for cars, appliances, major car repairs, children's college, or retirement?

8. Are you unable to accumulate money for emergency situations?

9. Are you surprised when you see the amount of your credit card bill?

10. Do you make impulsive purchases? How often?

11. Do you frequently return things you've purchased?

12. Does spending money or shopping boost your spirits when you feel down in the dumps or after a disagreement with another person?

13. Do you ever lie about money to your spouse or partner?

14. Do you change the subject or become upset when your spouse or partner tries to discuss financial concerns with you?

15. Are you unable to say no to your child's or partner's requests?

16. Are you unable to say no to salespeople?

17. Do you have poor financial habits, such as overdrawing your bank accounts, not balancing your checkbook, paying bills late, excessively using ATM or debit cards, or avoiding filing income tax returns?

18. Do you try to influence other people's opinions of your financial situation, either by impressing others or downplaying your resources?

19. Do you build up debt, pay it off, promise not to repeat the debt, and do it again anyway?

20. Have you contemplated bankruptcy as a way to get out of your debt problems?

21. Have you taken out home equity loans or second mortgages to pay off your debts?

22. In general, do you see debt tools such as home equity loans, second mortgages, and bankruptcy as solutions to your problems?

Your answers to these questions will help you understand if you tend to be a compulsive spender in some form. If you answered yes to eight or more questions, it's likely that you have a problem with spending money. Your problem may manifest itself in different ways: through shopping, credit cards, or a lifelong pattern of debt.

HOARDING HABITS (HOARDERS)

1. Do you panic if your bank account drops below a certain amount?

2. Do you avoid replacing or repairing necessary items when they are broken?

3. Do you obsess over your bank balances and investment accounts?

4. Does your family complain that you are too tight with money?

5. Do your family members purchase items for you because you won't buy them for yourself?

6. Do you feel burdened by other people's demands on you for money?

7. Do you attempt to control your spouse's or partner's spending?

8. Do you frequently argue with your partner or family about spending money?

9. Have you paid bills late even though you had money in the bank?

10. Do you secretly feel superior to people who freely spend money?

Your answers to these questions will help you understand if you tend to be a hoarder. If you answered yes to four or more questions, it's likely that you suffer from financial obsession and hoarding behavior. Your relationship with money most likely affects those you love more than you realize.

MONEY AVERSION AND UNDERACHIEVEMENT HABITS (MONEY AVERTERS AND FINANCIAL UNDERACHIEVERS)

1. Do you avoid asking for a raise?

2. Do you know your monthly expenses?

3. Do you have credentials or skills that you are not making use of?

4. Do others with your skills or experience make more money than you?

5. Do you believe that you are living a downscaled or simpler life by choice?

6. Do you own a business that is unable to issue you a regular paycheck?

7. If you are self-employed, do you avoid focusing on your profit until you file your income taxes?

8. Are you passive and avoidant about pursuing money that is owed you?

9. Are you concerned that others won't like you if you ask them to pay their share?

10. Do you rely on a partner, your parents, or your siblings to lend you money for basic necessities?

11. Did you avoid moving from your parents' home longer than your peers?

Your answers to these questions will help you understand if you tend to be a financial averter or underachiever. If you answered yes to five or more questions, it's likely that you are most comfortable depriving yourself and avoiding financial matters. Because you have been unwilling to concern yourself with financial matters, you are probably in debt.

FINANCIAL DEPENDENCE HABITS (FINANCIAL DEPENDENTS AND VIOLATORS)

1. Do you believe you are incapable of supporting yourself financially?

2. Are you fearful of financial responsibilities?

3. If you are married or living together in a permanent long-term relationship, were you attracted to your partner because you felt he or she could provide for you?

4. If you are single, do you actively pursue someone because you believe he or she will provide for you?

5. Do you put all the responsibility for your joint finances on your partner?

6. Do you think financial areas of life are too complicated for you to understand?

7. Do you secretly wish that someone would save you from your financial situation?

8. Do you manipulate people to give you things?

9. Do you feel that you deserve special financial benefits?

10. Do you feel entitled to special financial treatment?

11. Do you think other people owe you?

12. Is it hard for you to understand people who tell the truth on income tax returns?

Your answers to these questions will help you understand if you tend to expect others to provide financial support or opportunities for you. If you answered yes to four or more questions, it's likely that relationships tend to center around your financial dependence, or if you are a financial violator, you scheme to manipulate circumstances for your own advancement.

Severity and Progression

As you acquaint yourself with your particular financial habits, you'll need to determine the severity and progression of your situation. Take some time to reflect on and answer the following questions.

1. Which specific behaviors are especially problematic for you?

2. Which ones do you think are abnormal?

3. Which ones do you wish you could stop?

4. Has anyone else ever commented about these behaviors?

5. What negative consequences have you experienced related to:

    a. spending too much?

    b. shopping excessively?

    c. shopping and then returning items?

    d. hoarding money or things?

    e. being unable to spend money, even when it was critical and you had enough?

    f. not earning enough money to live on?

    g. expecting others to provide for you?

6. What steps have you taken to try to stop that have not worked?

7. How have these behaviors grown worse over time?

Your answers to the above questions will help you determine whether your behaviors and your financial problems have escalated. As you recall, we learned in chapter 2 that these problems tend to get worse over time, despite attempts to improve and despite negative consequences. If, no matter what you do, your problematic use of money continues to get worse, it's likely that you've slipped into addiction territory.

❖

These assessment questions are designed for you to take an honest look at yourself and your current money behaviors. After reflecting on the vast array of money behaviors, where do you think you fit? Do you believe you lean more toward spending, dependence, hoarding, or underachievement? How severe do you think your problem is? Do you think those close to you have money addictions? If you are still unclear, you may also choose to do the assessment from Debtors Anonymous, listed in appendix B (page 185).

Admitting that you have a problem is a great beginning. In the next section, the assessment questions will help you recognize the roots of this problem, so you can begin to help yourself.

Understanding Your Money History

As you recall from chapter 3, financial legacies are passed from generation to generation. Asking yourself the following questions will enable you to reflect on your family's money patterns and begin to see how your financial blueprint was formed. You'll start to see patterns in how your specific behaviors replicate your parents' beliefs about money, as well as the monetary dealings that you witnessed.

How You Handled Money as a Child

Your relationship with money as a child develops out of a variety of circumstances, including financial stress, a parent's or sibling's addiction, trauma, family status, how you perceived yourself within your family, learning disabilities, and school difficulties. The following questions trace the origins of problematic money behaviors.

YOUR FAMILY'S FINANCIAL CIRCUMSTANCES

1. What was the financial status of your family in comparison to your relatives or the neighborhood—rich, poor, or average?

2. Was there great wealth?

3. Were there periods of poverty when basic physical needs were not met?

4. Was there financial upheaval or hardship caused by illness, addictions, or divorce?

5. Were there financial losses or large, unforeseeable events that devastated the family finances?

6. Who earned the money?

7. Who spent the money?

YOUR EARLY FINANCIAL CIRCUMSTANCES

1. Did you have an allowance?

2. Did you have trouble not spending money?

3. Did you stash or hoard money?

4. Did you frequently borrow money from parents, siblings, or friends?

5. Did you ever steal money from someone close to you?

6. Were there inequities between you and your siblings in allowances or financial privileges?

7. Were you envious of your friends' possessions?

8. Did you experience a frequent sense of longing for better things?

9. Did you think your parents were fair in their financial dealings with you?

10. Did people close to you often make promises about money that they didn't keep?

YOUR PARENTS' FINANCIAL BEHAVIORS

1. Based on what you've read in the first five chapters, do you think one or both of your parents or caregivers had dysfunctional money habits?

2. What were your parents' specific concerns about money?

3. How did your mother relate to money? What do you think she believed about money?

4. How did your father relate to money? What do you think he believed about money?

5. How did your parents handle disagreements or differences about money?

6. How often did your parents argue about money?

7. Were your parents satisfied with their financial circumstances?

8. Were your parents concerned about status or possessions?

9. How did your parents cope if they couldn't afford things they wanted?

10. Did you ever worry about your family's financial circumstances?

11. Did your parents steal money or possessions from you?

12. What did your parents teach you about money management?

13. Did your parents pressure you to succeed financially or expect you to surpass them in economic status?

14. Do you think your parents unconsciously competed with you or needed you to fail financially?

YOUR PARENTS' COPING MECHANISMS

1. What method did your parents use when faced with stress and hardship?

2. If your parents had financial difficulties, did they deny the situation?

3. When there was financial conflict, did they avoid discussing it?

4. Were you aware that your parents kept secrets about financial problems?

5. Did either of your parents boast about or focus a lot of attention on financial security?

6. Did your parents put a lot of attention on managing the family image?

7. Did your parents hoard money or material goods?

INTERGENERATIONAL INFLUENCES

1. What do you know about your grandparents' financial story?

2. What do you know about how your parents, grandparents, or great-grandparents coped with the Great Depression?

3. Do you have any of the following in your family history?

   a. Immigrants?

   b. Refugees?

   c. Survivors of catastrophes (e.g., slavery, the Holocaust, Japanese American internment, Native American oppression, Armenian diaspora, Cambodian genocide)?

4. Did money come between your parents and their siblings?

5. Did your ancestors experience sudden financial loss or gain?

These family history questions are all designed to help you gain insight into your past and the family patterns that still shape you today. In the next section, you'll learn how you can benefit from this insight.

How to Learn from Your Family History

Whether you are experiencing a few financial problems, a money addiction, or trouble due to a loved one's money habits, the questions you've just answered have helped raise your awareness of how you got to be who you are today. Further on, we'll explore treatment and recovery. For now, take a few moments to assimilate what you've learned about yourself through these questions—and why it's important.

Exploring family history helps both addicts and codependents. This history gives insight into the financial precursors to addictive behaviors. Speaking about your family history makes it more real to you and thus helps break down denial. Moreover, it helps you connect your current behaviors to the underpinnings of those behaviors. As you begin to reflect on your behavior patterns, you'll feel invigorated and motivated to engage in the healing process.

This may be the first time you've actually looked at your history with money. In a culture where it is considered impolite to talk about money, typically no one has ever asked before. Most likely you've probably wanted to open up and talk about family history when given the opportunity. The conversation is a relief. You want to say, "At last! Somebody wants to hear the craziness of my story and it's okay to tell it."

Speaking about both your own and your family's money patterns will help you to break free from the bonds of your family legacy. As you break free, you'll no longer be driven to live up to someone else's ideals, act out someone else's unfulfilled dreams or pain, or reenact trauma that is sometimes generations old. You'll be free to discover what is truly important to you and find your own financial health.

❖

Now that you have a better understanding of how to use your family history to understand your present-day behaviors, take another break to review your current behaviors, your family patterns, and how they might connect.

Summary

With the aid of these assessment tools, you'll be on your way to understanding whether you have a money problem or money addiction, and what the problem's origins might be. If after reviewing the questions thus far you feel that you have serious problems with money—perhaps an addiction or a troubled relationship with a money addict—don't despair. There's hope! Many people have learned how to improve their lives. The next chapters will help you learn more about how you can, too.

• • •

Beginning Recovery

Make no mistake: recovery from money problems and money addiction is tough.

Recovery begins when you can no longer deny to yourself that you are powerless over your own behavior. You finally reach a low point (you "hit bottom") and are forced to admit that you can't continue like this. Chances are your low point is precipitated by a financial crisis. Maybe you don't have the rent money or you owe back taxes to the IRS. Maybe your partner gave you an ultimatum.

Even if you aren't in immediate crisis or haven't hit bottom yet, you may be close. Better to begin now than later. Getting out of crisis mode might take several months, so be patient with yourself as you attempt some new behaviors. And there's a lot to do. In the early stages of recovery, you have to handle your current monetary pressures at the same time that you plan for future financial obligations.

In recovery, you will learn to pay attention to your finances, perhaps more than you ever have. This is necessary because money is such an essential part of life. When a person is recovering from drug, alcohol, or gambling addictions, the goal is to completely stop using the addictive substance. But you can't do that with money, so you have to learn to pay close attention to specific details about money usage.

As you recall from chapter 4, there are many types of problem users and money addicts, and they relate to money matters in four ways: indulging, obsessing, depriving, and avoiding. Only one type, the person who obsessively deprives herself—also called a hoarder—is usually *not* in debt, and because of this doesn't feel the pain of hitting bottom and doesn't attempt to change or seek help. Families of hoarders are the ones who suffer from the hoarder's deprivation. The three other types usually have tremendous financial pressure and debt. Their negative consequences and pain lead them to seek help. This book will address how the change process is different for money addicts who are in debt and those who are not in debt. However, it is rare for a hoarder to seek help.

 IF YOU ARE TRULY AN ADDICT, IT GOES WITHOUT SAYING THAT YOU CAN'T DO THIS ALONE. YOU WILL NEED TO PUT INTO ACTION THE GUIDANCE FROM THIS BOOK, DRAW ON THE SUPPORT OF GOOD FRIENDS AND FAMILY, AND GET INVOLVED IN A GOOD SUPPORT PROGRAM.

Many of you reading this book will fall into the category of problem user—that is, you aren't a full-blown money addict. You may find enough help in this book to get yourself to a place of health, though it still would be helpful for you to seek assistance. If you are truly an addict, it goes without saying that you can't do this alone. You will need to put into action the guidance from this book, draw on the support of good friends and family, and get involved in a good support program, such as Debtors Anonymous. Therapists trained in addictions are also helpful. Support resources are available in appendix D (page 219).

Whether you're a problem user or a money addict, let's take a look at what recovery will be like for you.

Six Phases of Recovery

There are six phases of recovery from money problems. A brief overview of these six phases follows.

Phase 1: Hitting Bottom

You may be at or near this point now. You feel emotional pain, financial pressure, or both. You are not sure, but you are beginning to recognize that your behavior is the source of this pain. You become more aware of all the ways you deny your problem—the rationales, excuses, and twisted logic that have kept you overindulging or depriving yourself and others. You'll learn more about phase 1 in this chapter.

Phase 2: Accepting and Following Guidance

You begin to climb out of the destructive spiral you've been in. But you aren't in this alone. This book (and other people you may be working with) will give you direction, and your job is to follow that direction—and to take action. Despite your best intentions, if you aren't willing to take direction and try out new behaviors, you will remain stuck in your problems. You need to become accountable and tell the truth about your situation to another person, possibly a family member, spouse or partner, financial planner, or Twelve Step sponsor. You commit to a life that involves healthy behavior toward money. Phase 2 and accompanying actions for you to take are discussed in this chapter.

Phase 3: Creating a Life Vision

You've been indulging or depriving yourself based on old patterns and psychic wounds—many from your childhood and some that may have been passed from generation to generation. Healthy money management *begins* by developing your own life vision. This life vision will enable you to maintain motivation for the hard work ahead. You, more than anyone, need a larger purpose to make changes, because addicts are focused on present-day fixes. A life vision helps you realize that there's more to life than going to the mall, paying off debts, and keeping the bill collectors at bay—or, if you're a hoarder, putting yet one more dollar in your savings account. *Recovery is about aligning with deeper meanings in life.* In phase 3, which is discussed in chapter 8, you'll create a life vision with personal and financial goals.

Phase 4: Living with a Spending Plan

You will be more successful with recovery if you have both tools and a plan. In phase 4, you learn beginning tools to develop a spending plan, including paperwork organization, stopping credit card use, and record keeping. The spending plan is the cornerstone of financial recovery, guiding you toward healthy spending. Indulgers will learn to curtail spending to keep to a plan. The spending plan helps determine spending choices, guides the flow of cash in your life, and accounts for inevitable slips into old behaviors. It is your magic carpet, taking you places you only dreamed of before. This phase is covered in chapter 8.

Phase 5: Changing Your Thinking, Feelings, and Impulsive Actions

Normal money managers can be given financial tools and be on their way to change. Problematic money managers, however, need additional support in order to sustain change. This phase helps you to recognize your dysfunctional thinking and guides you toward more wholesome, positive problem solving. In phase 5 you'll also learn methods to cope with difficult feelings in constructive ways and to manage your impulsive actions with money. Equipped with a full repertoire of skills, you are better able, whether an indulger or a depriver, to handle the fluctuations of your finances. Phase 5 and action steps are discussed in chapter 9.

Phase 6: Living the Abundant Life

Abundance is not solely about money; it's a perspective. You now have the skills to handle life's ups and downs without feeling that your financial security is threatened. Your former behaviors do not guide your decisions. Indulgers have learned what's necessary to handle inner desires, impulses, and emergencies. Deprivers have learned to let go and derive pleasure from using and sharing money. Both indulgers and deprivers now understand that true worth comes from inside a person. Now that financial pressure and worry are not foremost in your life, you are free to make deliberate financial decisions leading to greater life satisfaction. You discover and embrace your authentic lifestyle and purpose. Some of your life vision has become real. You may choose to continue to tackle childhood psychological, emotional, and spiritual issues surrounding money, but it isn't as crucial at this point for recovery. This phase is described in chapter 10.

❖

Recovery is not a linear process. Even though it's presented here as a series of clear steps, most likely you'll proceed at your own pace and your own circuitous fashion. Each of these phases can be adapted for your particular circumstances.

Phase 1: Hitting Bottom

Hitting bottom can happen gradually, or it can happen overnight.

Awareness of the financial crisis can arise gradually as the pain and pressure of being unable to pay bills and hiding your troubled relationship with money mounts over years. Gradually, you come to see that the negative consequences of your behavior outweigh the payoffs.

Hitting bottom can also come suddenly when, for instance, your spouse threatens divorce, your car is repossessed, or you can't pay for a medical problem. You are up against a wall with nowhere to turn. You may feel tremendous anxiety, panic, and hopelessness.

Samantha is a perfect example. Her husband kicked her out of the house after he discovered yet another $30,000 on the credit cards. He had already bailed her out of $55,000 in credit card debt eighteen months earlier. This time, he refused. His own dream of living without debt was long gone. Samantha agreed to enter therapy. She is making progress on her addictive spending, but her marriage may not survive.

For an indulger, typical ways of hitting bottom include one or more of the following:

- Foreclosure on home
- Repossession of a vehicle
- Being turned down by credit card companies
- Inability to borrow money from family or friends
- Phone calls from creditors
- Confrontation by a partner; being told to move out
- Inability to pay ordinary expenses, such as rent, mortgage, or groceries
- Arrest for embezzling or theft or other illegal activities

If you are a depriver, you hit bottom gradually as you experience increasing embarrassment and humiliation about finances. Some examples of these situations follow:

- Parents stop lending money to cover your basic living expenses.
- Chronic unemployment keeps you from renting or buying a home; you frequently move in with friends or relatives.

- Because you're not advancing in your career, you can't keep up with peers.

- Friends talk sarcastically about your hoarding or other money behavior.

- Your spouse threatens divorce because of the way you hoard money or the way you refuse to work to your ability.

- You lose connection with your grown children because of hoarding behavior.

Breaking through Denial

People with money problems can stay in denial for a long time. Because society condones dysfunctional financial behavior, it's easy to pretend that you are normal. Second, it's still considered impolite to speak about money, so the person with the problem doesn't want to tell anyone, and family and friends don't want to bring it up, either. Being in denial prevents you from understanding the full extent of the financial damage.

You pretend to know your financial situation even when you have barely looked at it. You probably skirt conversations about and references to money problems. You may avoid opening the mail, balancing your checkbook, thinking about expenses, or examining the total debt picture. And if you are a depriver, you actually believe that your behavior does not affect anyone but yourself, so you never ask.

With recovery from money problems, you can't fool around. If you want relief, you're going to need to stop pretending to yourself. The way to change is to stop pretending to yourself that you "can handle it," or "it isn't that bad," or "my problems don't affect anyone but me." The lies that worked before— whether lies you told others or lies you told yourself—have failed. You'll probably have to ask others in your life how your money behavior affects them, and you'll probably need some help.

Looking straight at the wreckage of your tangled finances forces you to face the problem. This is painful, but it's short-term pain, *as compared to what happens when you continue dysfunctional, self-destructive behavior.* If you allow yourself to experience the painful bottom, it helps you begin recovery and avoid causing further damage. Meanwhile, continuing these behaviors blocks you from fulfilling your future dreams.

For example, Sharon, a fifty-four-year-old, fashionably dressed woman, had never realized that her preoccupation with hoarding money had concerned anyone but herself. In fact, Sharon believed that saving a lot of money benefited her family. Sharon didn't allow her daughter to participate in school activities when a fee was involved. When her daughter turned seventeen, she announced that she wasn't going to college because she didn't want to burden the family with the expense. This announcement by her daughter was the beginning of Sharon's hitting bottom. She had wanted her daughter to go to college. She saw that her intense frugality and financial obsession had stunted her child's life choices. Her bright, talented daughter had absorbed a message that she wasn't worth college!

Questions in the following section, "Telling the Truth," also help you to see your situation more realistically.

Telling the Truth

Admitting the ways and the number of times you have sabotaged your own financial health is exceedingly difficult. The following questions are for both indulgers and deprivers. Take some time to answer them in your notebook or journal; it's an avenue for you to uncover the truth about your behavior.

- What do you consider dysfunctional about your money behaviors?
- How long have you been doing things like this?
- What do you think will happen if you keep going like this? You'll file for bankruptcy? Your spouse or partner will leave? You'll become a homeless bag person?
- How have you tried to change? How have your efforts helped you?
- Can you outline your whole financial situation?
- Do you have a list of your debts and monthly financial obligations?
- Have you ever asked your family how your money patterns affect them? What do you think they'd say?
- Are you willing to inform your family members about your financial situation?

When you begin to acknowledge the truth and expose your secrets, it's often excruciating. Yet this admission results in relief, a lessening of shame, and the first sense of hope that you can begin to take constructive action—real action, not just another promise that you'll break. Later in this chapter, we'll outline specific methods to help you tell the truth about your situation, including a worksheet for listing your debts and a thumbnail sketch worksheet of financial commitments.

Learning about Powerlessness and Addiction

You've hit bottom, and you've started to realize your need to tell the truth. Now you need to learn about the nature of powerlessness and your troubled relationship with money.

Seeing yourself as someone with a serious money problem or an addiction usually comes as a surprise; the concept is not yet part of the public consciousness. Most likely, you still falsely believe that if you had discipline and willpower, you could control your behavior. So it's surprising to think that things could be as bad as an addiction. And yet you might be relieved to know there's a name for your problem.

 TWELVE STEP PROGRAMS ARE INVALUABLE IN TREATING ADDICTIONS BECAUSE DENIAL, SECRECY, AND HIDING ARE LESSENED IN A GROUP FILLED WITH OTHERS STRUGGLING WITH THE SAME THOUGHTS AND BEHAVIORS.

The usual treatment for addiction involves therapy in conjunction with additional support—typically, the Twelve Step program Debtors Anonymous, which is based on Alcoholics Anonymous. Twelve Step programs are invaluable in treating addictions because denial, secrecy, and hiding are lessened in a group filled with others struggling with the same thoughts and behaviors. These groups help addicts recognize how their behaviors have grown worse over time and how they have not been able to stop or control their behavior for any significant length of time on their own. In these groups, addicts often begin to see how their actions are truly ruining their lives—and how the discipline of following a Twelve Step program can be the path to recovery. Even if you are not a full-blown money addict but consider yourself to be having serious debt and money problems, Debtors Anonymous can be very helpful. You will find other people there who have admitted that they were powerless over their money behaviors and who have chosen to improve their conduct with money.

Currently, you are blind to what's obvious to others: your money-related behaviors control you. In fact, your behavior is out of control. As tough as the reality of your situation is, you can get out of your financial quagmire by taking small, manageable steps. Even as you continue to struggle with your addictive impulses, you must be continually reminded that you are powerless over your thoughts and actions in and of themselves without the support of other recovering people, a Higher Power, and meetings to assist in the recovery process. This is why it is critical that you join a Twelve Step program such as Debtors Anonymous, where you can be with and learn from others who struggle with feeling powerless, too. These groups promise a way out for those who are willing to try.

Phase 2: Accepting and Following Guidance

Shame often accompanies the exposure of financial shortcomings. You need to tell these secrets to get help and overcome the shame. So think of what person in your life could help you, someone you can trust with the information. This can be a family member, friend, or Twelve Step sponsor. If you don't know such a person, consider someone in the helping professions: a priest, financial adviser, or therapist whom you trust. This financial helpmate will give you feedback about what he or she observes from your situation. Don't beat around the bush, make excuses for yourself, or avoid talking about how bad the situation is. Distorting your situation to others is a disservice you do to yourself, because it's just a matter of time before real circumstances punish you further for your problematic behavior. You don't have to solve your financial problems alone; in fact you won't be able to make lasting change unless you let someone in to help you. No one can help you unless you share your situation.

Allowing another person to see your financial records with you will reveal the extent of your problematic behaviors. You'll probably be unconsciously tempted to distort or withhold some information about your living expenses, debt load, and income. Prepare to tell your truth anyway, knowing that as you emerge from denial, you will recall additional expenses or commitments. Being honest, both with yourself or another, is a process and takes time. Eventually you'll realize that your life improves in proportion to your honesty.

To come out of the fog of denial you also need to learn to talk directly about specific numbers. The numbers do not lie; they have a story to tell, and if looked at without judgment or shame, the numbers will profoundly alter your denial system. Get the reality of your financial situation down on paper so you can see it. You can't hide from the numbers; they are the result of your choices. Look at them, and remember that regardless of how dire the circumstances look, there is always hope for change and recovery.

Be careful of perfectionist or black-and-white thinking. You might believe that you are not successful unless you are perfect and make grand efforts to change. Because you tend to think this way, you disregard your small steps and successes. Recovery requires you to lean on and accept the support of others—your therapist, your Twelve Step sponsor, or anyone else who is giving you guidance. As you share small successes, you will also be building trust. You'll need this trust, because no one is perfect and most addicts slip from their recovery plan. Without support to get you back on track, you can easily reenter the cycle of addiction as a response to your slip.

 RECOVERY REQUIRES YOU TO LEAN ON AND ACCEPT THE SUPPORT OF OTHERS—YOUR THERAPIST, YOUR TWELVE STEP SPONSOR, OR ANYONE ELSE WHO IS GIVING YOU GUIDANCE.

Consider Tracy, a fifty-three-year-old spending addict who has had three months of therapy for her money-related problems. In that time, she accelerated her car payments and made great headway on other debts. When her son was leaving for college, she suddenly decided that she needed to buy a bigger car to accommodate his belongings on the trips to his out-of-state school. In her relapse, Tracy did not discuss this potential purchase with her therapist; she just went out and bought the car. Typical of addicts, she hadn't considered the increased payments and what they would do to her progress on the recovery plan. When her therapist challenged her about how she intended to pay the additional $300 monthly car payment, Tracy replied that she had not really thought about the money and hadn't considered any other solution for moving her son back and forth from college.

Tracy truly believed that buying a big car—one she'd need only twice a year—was the correct choice. Her love of material objects confused her thinking. Tracy could not expand her options to include borrowing or renting a van twice a year for the next four years, cheaper options than buying a new vehicle outright.

She simply could not think this way on her own. This is typical of people with money problems. They often cannot think of alternate methods to solve problems. They act impulsively and believe that the manner in which they think is correct.

Tracy's therapist first complimented Tracy's positive *intent* to help out her son. The therapist then helped Tracy to see how this new financial commitment jeopardized the attainment of Tracy's other financial goals. The therapist accomplished this not by judging Tracy's relapse but by redirecting Tracy to the actual numbers in her spending plan and asking Tracy to reflect on how this purchase would get her closer to her goals. The therapist challenged Tracy, asking, "How will this choice help you to reach your goals?" Tracy looked at the hard facts and admitted that she'd slipped.

Relapses such as these are very common in recovery. And because they are common, learning to accept and follow guidance is a key task of recovery. Your job is to follow the steps outlined in this book. Trust your support network, and trust the process. Recovery will follow.

Action Steps

Whether you are an indulger who spends compulsively or a depriver who hoards obsessively, start with the following three steps: (1) gather financial statements, (2) stop credit card use, and (3) record all spending. These action steps require effort and blocks of time. You'll feel resistant because the actions are unfamiliar and difficult to execute at first. You might want to be perfect, but perfection is not the goal. Willingness to take direction and try new things is the goal. So do the best you can to start with the following actions.

STEP 1. GATHER FINANCIAL STATEMENTS

Gather your financial paperwork: a list of debts, bank statements, credit card statements, and so forth. You may have avoided looking at these documents for weeks, months, or even years because the bills are painful to face, especially if there has been little money to pay them. Some money addicts have unopened bills and credit card statements spread throughout their home. If so, it may take you several weeks to collect everything.

Initially, you don't need to review them or even open the bills. Simply gather them together in one central, convenient location. A shoebox will do to begin. (Eventually you will need a larger space, such as a file box or drawer dedicated to financial records or color-coded files.) For now, just begin to gather them, and start your new habit of organizing your papers.

With time, you'll need ongoing systems for keeping these papers together. Receipts, paid bills, and unpaid invoices and statements easily get lost in piles of junk mail or are stuffed randomly into "out of sight" locations. So you need your own method to steer your financial papers toward this central location. Think of temporary holding locations that you can utilize to house the many financial papers that come to you every day. Determine logical and convenient spots to temporarily place them until they reach their final destination. Some obvious places are a wallet, purse, designated pocket in your backpack, checkbook, daily planner, or designated desk drawer. Or place an envelope or bin in the spot where your money papers naturally gravitate. Use these temporary places, where financial documents collect until they are transferred to their permanent storage spot, consistently enough so that using them develops into a habit.

Note: This step is a bit different for those of you who are hoarders. Typically, hoarders are preoccupied with financial statements and bank balances, so this gathering and organization step is probably already accomplished. If you are a hoarder, your recovery task in step 1 is to *let the bills sit until they need to be paid,* perhaps once or twice a month. Don't open them and don't look at them until then.

Chart 7-1 on the next page lists the papers you need to collect in one spot. (A copy of this form is provided in the reproducible journal.)

The gathering process sets the stage to create a future organizational and filing system for financial papers. Healthy recovery requires that you respect and keep track of your important financial documents. It is healthy self-care for addicts to maintain clean and orderly financial files. You will need these documents later when you develop a realistic plan for debt repayment and spending, covered in chapter 8.

Once you have gathered the papers, you are ready to fill in the Debt Worksheet on page 103. Do this without judging yourself. It might be painful to see the numbers in black and white. Feeling this pain will motivate you to change. So list your debts without judging yourself. Your debts don't define

CHART 7-1

Documentation List

Type of Document	Found	Looked for but not found
Bank statements for current year		
Checkbook registers or duplicate checks for current year		
Credit card statements		
Outstanding bills: doctor, utilities, etc.		
Other financial contracts or obligations: car lease agreements, cell phone, cable TV, magazine subscriptions, etc.		
List of additional planned purchases and/or expenses for the next year: vacation, weddings, skis, conferences, etc.		
List of replacement purchases for the next year: new furnace, washer, roof, car tires, new car, etc.		

Notes:

you. You are not a good person or a bad person because of your debts. You are a person who wants to improve your financial circumstances, and in order to accomplish that, you will need to know the truth about your finances.

Consider going somewhere pleasant to fill in this form: a coffee shop, a library, or an outdoor park. Or consider inviting someone to sit with you while you transfer the information to the Debt Worksheet, shown in chart 7-2. (A second blank copy can be found in appendix C on page 189 or in the reproducible journal.) Choose someone you trust—a family member, friend, therapist, sponsor, or coach. Take a break and relax after you have filled in the form. Congratulations: this is the beginning of a fun journey. It only gets better from here.

STEP 2. STOP CREDIT CARD USE

The most important thing you can do for your recovery is to stop using credit cards. Nothing else will work until you stop pretending that you can afford things just because you have a credit card. Healthy money managers do not buy things when they do not have the money to pay for them. This is simple, old-fashioned commonsense logic: if you don't have the money in the bank, you can't buy anything. However, if you have a problematic or addictive relationship with money, you don't operate with common sense for two reasons. First, though you have an intellectual understanding that you shouldn't buy things you can't afford, you are still *powerless* over the addictive impulses. You just want to spend money because you want to spend money; having the money to pay is secondary. Second, in a culture where having credit cards and being in debt is the norm, saving to make a purchase no longer seems like common sense. (I should say, it is *sensible,* but it is no longer *common!*) Banking institutions and aggressive marketing tactics lead people to believe that purchasing on credit is what is *normal.*

Remember, it is financial good sense and *normal money management* to resist purchases unless you have available cash for that purchase. This is an important commitment to make. When you stop using credit cards, you demonstrate your willingness to change. Refraining from purchases you don't have the money for will empower you in your new lifestyle. These cards need to be cut up and the accounts should be closed.

Here's why.

CHART 7-2

Debt Worksheet

Debt	Total Amount Due	Finance Charge (Percent)	Minimum Payments	Date of Last Payment	Other Comments
Credit Cards					
Other Debts					
Car Loan #1					
Car Loan #2					
Equity Line #1					
Equity Line #2					
Utilities					

CHART 7-2

Debt Worksheet (continued)

Debt	Total Amount Due	Finance Charge (Percent)	Minimum Payments	Date of Last Payment	Other Comments
Medical Bills					
Services					
Personal Debts					
TOTAL					

Debt increases your financial obligations for the future. In this way, *debt reduces your future choices.* When you accrue a balance on a credit card, you "borrow" from your own future. In the future, you will still have the same living expenses—only now you add a loan payment to your regular bills. If you are a problem user or money addict and you increase your debt, you continue to deny the reality of tomorrow's expenses. This is counter to the goal of healthy financial planning, which tries to ensure that tomorrow's expenses will be covered. Accruing debt takes you in the direction opposite where you want to be. It absolutely ensures fewer options for tomorrow. When you are in debt, you become a person whose life focuses on digging out of a hole. You can only see the walls closed in around you. In contrast, when you have savings, it's like standing on top of a mountain; there are many choices available all around you.

 CREDIT CARD COMPANIES ARE WELL AWARE THAT PEOPLE SPEND MORE READILY AND IMPULSIVELY WHEN PAYING WITH PLASTIC THAN WITH CASH.

Buying with credit cards encourages impulsive spending. Credit card companies are well aware that people spend more readily and impulsively when paying with plastic than with cash.

It is easier to stay in denial about how much you are spending when using plastic to pay. Even though plastic is a preferred method of payment, it doesn't feel like you are really spending money because the payment is delayed. It's also easier to stay in denial about how individual purchases accrue to your total debt load. When pressured by the balance, most money addicts obtain additional cards. Additional credit cards extend the bottoming-out process.

Many people with money problems only pay the minimum balance. The trouble is that, even if you stop using them, credit cards take a long time—about thirty years—to pay off with minimum payments. This increases the cost of your purchases. Think about whether you like what you are buying enough to pay for it for thirty years.

Debit cards and ATM cards present the same problems. Plain and simple, plastic money promotes denial about spending. Because of this denial, if you are someone who has problematic money habits, *you cannot handle paying with plastic of any sort.* If you are one of these people, debit cards are just like credit cards and often lead to overdrawing an account. These overdrafts are expensive; the Center for Responsible Lending reported that Americans now pay $17.5 billion annually for debit card overdraft fees.[1] When you overdraw your bank account, you are left with the same psychological debilitation as with increased debt. If you have a problem with money, you typically don't have an accurate sense of bank balances; thus you should not be using credit, debit, or ATM cards. If you do use a debit card, you need to record the transactions immediately in your check register and think of them as cash, with the money coming out of the account right now.

You probably feel resistant to the idea of not using credit cards for any purchase whatsoever. Some people believe they can't do it. It takes time to be willing to discontinue using credit cards. But you must stop using the credit cards and then close the accounts if you want to make progress in diminishing your overall debt load. A sinking boat cannot be bailed out if it still has a hole in it. You have to close the leak first. Unless the hole is completely closed up, it's all too common for a problem user to clear the slate with sweeping gestures like home equity lines, only to begin the process again.

You may have panic and withdrawal just thinking about life without these cards. This withdrawal is not physiologically based, but it is as powerful as withdrawing from a chemical substance. If so, try self-care techniques until the urges subside. You may need to make phone calls several times a day to your support team, your sponsor, or your therapist for a period of time.

 IF YOU HAVE A PROBLEM WITH MONEY, YOU TYPICALLY DON'T HAVE AN ACCURATE SENSE OF BANK BALANCES; THUS YOU SHOULD NOT BE USING CREDIT, DEBIT, OR ATM CARDS.

You might argue that you *need* a safety net, one credit card for emergencies. Credit cards, a normal tool for payment, are also the easiest method of payment. Even financially responsible citizens now believe that credit cards are *necessary* for emergencies and for building credit. However, in healthy financial planning, emergencies are rare occurrences. Natural catastrophes such as hurricanes, earthquakes, or tornadoes are emergencies. Tragic health problems are emergencies. Healthy money managers save for emergencies and recognize that everything they own will break down. *Savings* cover those breakdowns, not credit cards.

It is *not* an emergency when the brakes on your car need replacing. Because brakes wear down, it's a normal, predictable expense. It is *not* an emergency when the washing machine requires repairs. Root canals are *not* financial emergencies, because teeth wear out. Wedding gifts for your children are *not* emergencies. A new water heater is *not* an emergency.

It's imperative to recognize that you need savings to repair and/or replace your possessions. Technological and mechanical items particularly will be replaced or updated. You also need to plan for upcoming life events, such as deteriorating health and other expenses of aging. All of these expenses should be predicted and planned for; they are a normal part of life and happen to everyone.

Truly if *credit cards are needed for emergencies,* then the card would only be used when real emergencies occur, perhaps once or twice a decade. You would use the card and not use it again until the next emergency. You have a problem and are rationalizing your credit card use if you can't keep to these rare occasions. If you have a money problem or a money addiction, you should not be using them at all, because for you, the *emergency* use of the card often leads to more use.

It's okay to stop using them at your own pace. However, if you don't stop immediately, you should discuss every additional credit card purchase that you make with a trusted person—your spouse or partner, sponsor, or therapist. It's important to be accountable to another person about this. Some helpful techniques are listed below:

- Give the credit card to your partner or a trusted friend to be "saved" until you are ready to close the account.

- Commit to writing and mailing an additional check immediately to the credit card company if you "slip" and use the credit card. This will prevent an accumulation of additional balances.

- Put a sticker on your credit card with the balance due on it, to remind yourself of your total debt when you use it.

- Clip a picture of your life vision to the credit card as a reminder of future goals.

- Keep a positive credit balance on the credit card; use it like a debit card.

It is challenging to speak to representatives at these credit card companies. They are trained to badger customers to keep the account open. They make it difficult for you by offering other possibilities. If you are unprepared for this onslaught of high-pressure sales, you are likely to be intimidated and unsuccessful. Prepare for this hassle; ask someone to role-play or rehearse with you before making the phone calls. Arm yourself with debt statistics.

And then cut up those cards.

STEP 3. RECORD ALL SPENDING

In recovery, it's absolutely necessary to keep track of every dollar that you spend, including small amounts of cash. Without accurate financial records, there is no accountability and no information on which to base decisions. Tracking your cash spending is especially important because there is no paper trail. You receive paper statements from your checks, debit card, and credit card purchases, so those are easier to track. You can record your cash spending in your planner, on a three- by five-inch card in your wallet, in a small spiral-bound booklet, in a blank check register booklet, or anywhere else that's convenient for you.

Documenting your spending is time-consuming, and it may be a daunting exercise at first. Just keep at it; it becomes easier with practice. This is a crucial step, because all change begins with awareness. Keeping track of how and where you spend money will give you awareness about where your money is going. You may be good at deceiving yourself, but the written numbers won't lie. As you record this, you'll start to understand where that twenty-dollar bill disappeared to. This is a quick way to come out of denial. It might be shocking to see the places where you hemorrhage money, as well as how it leaks and dribbles away. But you need to see it in order to change it. Difficult or not, if you want to change, you must do it; your recovery depends on it.

For some people, this awareness is very sobering. They are able to change immediately simply by seeing excessive spending in one category—dining out, for instance. Or you might notice that your outings with your children tend to cost more than you realized. Or at the end of the month, you may decide you are spending way too much on clothing and take a hiatus for a while.

Most problem users and all addicts don't want to see where the money goes and will resist this record-keeping step. You have to be relentless about writing down your expenditures. Even if your records aren't perfect, you must persist. You might forget to record some things, and that's okay. Don't judge it, just write it down.

Ultimately, this ongoing habit will help you to see whether your spending aligns with your values and life vision. Slowly and over time, you can assess whether what you are buying is what you truly want. You'll start to see how your impulsive spending created trouble in the first place and realize that continuing that pattern will prevent you from recovery.

Gathering your financial papers, stopping your use of credit and debit cards, and record keeping are concrete actions for you to begin immediately. In Twelve Step programs, this is called "footwork." You can also begin other actions, like calling one of your creditors to make payment arrangements, returning an unused and unnecessary item you recently purchased, talking to your partner or spouse about finances, or asking for a raise. These concrete steps help you stay motivated and focused on productive movement and change. Taking action decreases your anxiety and sense of hopelessness.

Remember, you cannot recover without behaving or acting differently. Your treatment is not about getting new insights into who you are. You will recover by changing your behaviors, and action plans are one such avenue for new behavior.

Summary

In this chapter, you learned about the six phases of recovery, and you focused on the first two: hitting bottom and accepting and following guidance. The first two phases of recovery are often emotionally draining. You may not be embarking on this journey because you want to. Perhaps you've reached a desperation point or realized that unless you change, you will lose people you love. Nevertheless, hitting bottom and learning to accept guidance involve soul-searching and practical attention to hard facts. The nitty-gritty facts, once laid bare, are the steps of recovery that lay the foundation for real change.

The next chapter continues with phases 3 and 4, which take the recovery process further into specific behavioral choices and strategies.

• • •

Life Visions and Spending Plans

This chapter outlines phases 3 and 4 of recovery. In the course of reading it, you will come to understand how to create a life vision and how to create a spending plan that aligns your finances with your life vision.

Phase 3: Creating a Life Vision

Healthy money management begins by getting clear about what you want and developing a life vision. A *life vision* is the fantasy of your ideal life. You probably fantasize about an ideal life without realizing it. This vision is a blueprint of your unique values and goals, and it illuminates your life purpose. Because no two people have exactly the same vision, no one but you can define it for you. The vision answers questions, such as "What would you do with your life if you never had to worry about money again?" and "If you could have everything you wanted, if you could be anything you wanted, if you could do whatever you wanted, what would that look like?"

When you develop your life vision, you aren't directly attempting money management; instead you aim to find your unique place in the Money Problems Matrix. This vision defines how important material acquisition is to you and how to better balance the interface between material (tangible) and spiritual (intangible) satisfaction. Some life dreams cost money to fulfill and others don't. Clarifying your life vision helps you recognize which dreams will require financial resources and which ones won't. With your life vision in hand, you are better equipped to keep motivation going when you have to discipline your spending. Whatever form your money problems take, the life vision awakens hope and frees you from despair. You'll learn to use your money for true life satisfaction.

So don't skip this step; there's more to financial recovery than accounting drudgery, paying off debts, and keeping the bill collectors at bay.

Step 1. Capture Your Fantasy

You can either write your life vision in your notebook or the reproducible journal, or share it with a friend, partner, or therapist. Allow yourself some special undisturbed time to spontaneously answer the following questions. Don't worry about getting it all the first time through; fantasies take time to unfold.

- If you had all the money in the world, what would you do?
- What do you want to have or do before you die?
- What would you do if you won the lottery?
- What do you imagine about your retirement? What activities are you hoping to begin after retirement?
- If a genie came out of a bottle, what magical wishes would you want granted?
- Have you seen lifestyles portrayed in movies or books that appeal to you?
- As a child, what fantasies did you have about your future?

Perhaps this process is fun, and exciting dreams are bubbling up. However, if you have never considered possibilities for yourself and this process is difficult, don't fret. It gets easier to fantasize each time you do it. It may be impossible for you to create a fantasy future, since money problems grow in emotionally unfertile soil. From the outside, it may have looked as if your life were fulfilling materialistic promises. The truth is that this lavish self-gratification was impulsive and void of thoughtful reflection about your values. Most likely, you have been using your money without mature awareness of your heart's true desires.

It's helpful to collect appealing images from magazines and construct collages from them to clarify your dreams. Do this spontaneously and without judging yourself. Just let yourself cut out every image that you like. After you get a stack of images, first look only at the *stuff* in the image. Second, take some time to reflect about why these particular images attracted you. What qualities are hiding behind the material objects? For example, at first glance you see a photo of a horse. Then with deeper reflection, you recall your childhood dreams of freedom or the desire to be connected to nature. Ask yourself why you are attracted to the images you selected.

FOR INDULGERS

If you are an indulger, you love to dream because it gives you permission to have everything without regard for payment. Often you'll surprise yourself when you realize it isn't things that you want. You might fantasize connections with people, or time in nature, or other less materialistic lifestyles. These fantasies will help you decipher the code of your values. Later, when you construct a spending plan, you'll know which categories can be eliminated and which can't. You'll also need to explore nonmaterial means to achieve the same feelings without actual purchases. People with money problems have a narrow vision about how to satisfy needs and are seldom discriminating in their choices. They may become fixated on certain fantasies or beliefs that objects or activities are what they "have to have," without ever asking what they *hope to gain* from these products. Driving a fancy new car is not going to make up for the embarrassment in third grade when your mother's car was repossessed in front of your friends. No car can ever heal that trauma. The person with a desire like this believes she needs the car when, in reality, she's never explored or gained insight into what the car represents.

If you are an indulger, ask yourself the following questions to discover what values lie beneath the objects you fantasize having. (Substitute the actual objects you desire for those in the list.) You may want to write the answers in your notebook or in the space provided in the journal.

- What will you feel when you're in that house?
- What does driving that fancy car say about you? Whom do you know who has a car like that? Why do you prefer that car instead of another one?
- What associations do you have with this object? Why is it important?
- How does it feel to have a cook, a gardener, and so on?

There is an underlying pattern to the things you want; you just haven't stopped long enough to think about what these things represent to you. For instance, James, a compulsive spender, owns four cars: two he's fixing up, one to drive to work every day, and one SUV for hunting trips with the guys. He insists he needs all of them, despite the financial hardship it causes. When he reflected on what the cars meant to him, he remembered working on cars with his grandfather as a teenager. He likes the four-wheel-drive SUV because he thinks of himself as an outdoor person, especially when he's with his buddies from high school. He says cars are like his toys; they remind him of when he had less stress.

James, like other compulsive spenders and debtors, is striving to recapture a special feeling from the past. It's just like a cocaine addict who wants to recapture that first high even though the next high is no longer fun and only brings more disasters.

Problem money users and money addicts are only aware of the urge, "I have to have it." They don't take the time to reflect on why these purchases mean so much. If you have been an indulger, you must take the time to discover the pattern that sits beneath your fantasies and acquisitions.

FOR DEPRIVERS

Those with the depriving addictions (financial underachievers, hoarders, and money averters) often don't know how to dream and see possibilities. If you are a depriver, you think the world has scarce or limited resources, so you try to *get by* or *make do.* You probably haven't ever allowed yourself time or energy to discover what you truly want. As a compensation for feeling deprived, you may either overspend or, conversely, you might say no to everything extra in life and be unable to see that material pleasure or comfort could be within your reach.

This is an opportunity to explore your childhood wounds. Because deprivation has become so natural to you, you need to develop financial fantasies. The fantasy might be having one satisfying, well-paying job instead of three part-time jobs without benefits. It may involve the possibility of simple vacations or feeling deserving of new, high-quality furniture rather than accepting used furniture.

You'll want to explore what "not having" has meant to you. You may fear owning nice possessions because your siblings don't have them and you were supposed to be the "Cinderella" sibling in your family. Do you deserve new shoes every three months? What would happen if you allowed yourself to buy two purebred cats rather than just taking in a stray cat? Ask yourself these questions:

- What would it say about you if you had more material wealth?

- What would happen if you spent money freely?

- What adult responsibility do you get to avoid by not having the ability to flex financial muscles?

- What will it say about you if you have a better job?

- Do you feel you deserve to replace a possession before the previous one isn't entirely used up or threadbare?

- Whom would you make happy and whom would you disappoint if you were more successful with finances?

You may need outside help to round out your fantasy because often key components can be missed. As you continue doing this, you'll gradually learn to think bigger and bigger and to see that you can surpass your self-imposed glass ceiling. Your obsessive deprivation doesn't allow you to see that you deserve to have a job close to home, or satisfying work, or an understanding boss. Get self-balancing help from someone who will ask questions to prompt you and open up a range of options.

At the outset of recovery, you won't be able to see the full range of options. Later in recovery, when you start to see that your dreams can come true, you'll be able to expand your original fantasy into new territory.

Step 2. Develop Personal and Financial/Material Goals

PERSONAL GOALS

Money is only one aspect of life and only a part of your financial recovery. Your overall life vision includes discovering who you are and what you want from life. This requires you to set specific nonmonetary goals. Answering these questions in your notebook or journal will help you think about your goals:

- What do you want to do with your life?

- As a youngster, what did you want to be when you grew up?

- What types of activities excite you? What activities excite you when you see others doing them or read about them in books or magazines?

- What's important for you to achieve in your lifetime?

- Is there anything you want to learn? History, economics, geography?

To play an instrument, speak a language, knit, lay brick pavers, install a garbage disposal, use a lathe, complete college, become a master gardener, or earn a certificate?

- Do you see yourself volunteering or doing any community service, such as teaching English as a second language or volunteering for the Red Cross, at hospitals, or for your favorite charity?

- What physical and health goals do you want to strive for? Think beyond the typical ones of losing weight and exercising regularly. Think about taking vitamins, completing a marathon, hiking a certain trail, cutting down on the fat in your diet, regularly doing exercises to help your back condition, or becoming a vegetarian.

- Are there relationships that you would like to work on, such as becoming closer to your parents or children, finding a new relationship or new friends, learning to talk with new acquaintances, or mending fences with a former spouse or partner?

- Is there a spiritual practice you would like to begin or resume, such as daily mediation, prayer, or finding a worship community?

- Would you like to do something adventurous or find a new activity for expanding your mind and your circle of friends? The possibilities could include belly dancing, sky diving, scuba diving, hot air balloon rides, reenacting the Civil War, geo-caching, woodworking, or genealogy.

- What would you like to give back to the world? What mark would you like to make after you are gone?

FINANCIAL/ MATERIAL GOALS

You also need to develop financial and material goals. List your long-term material goals in your notebook or in the space provided in the journal. Chart 8-1 shows some examples.

Make a list of these goals and put a dollar figure on each goal. Hopefully, these goals are fun to generate and easy to visualize.

CHART 8-1

Sample Long-Term Financial/Material Goals

Long-Term Goal	Estimated Cost	Estimated Date
Pay off all credit cards	$37,841	9 years
Save cash for a vacation	$1,000	2 years
Pay off mortgage		28 years
Take scuba lessons*	$175	Now
Buy a Jet Ski	$3,500	5 years
Save for retirement	$400/month	Starting in 1 year
Move to a bigger house	On hold	On hold
Remodel the basement	$15,000	After credit cards are paid off
Replace the furnace	$3,400	18 months
Reupholster Grandma's couch*	$1,400	6 months
Travel to a foreign country	$3,400	5 years
Donate more to charity	$50/month	Starting in 3 years

* These goals will be transferred to a list of short-term goals.
  See chart 8-2 on the next page.

Next make a list of short-term financial goals, including things you intend to purchase for the next twelve months. This list is more specific, as you can see in chart 8-2. When you made your list of long-term goals, you may have discovered that some of them may be reached in less than twelve months. Transfer them to your short-term goals list.

CHART 8-2

Sample Short-Term Financial/Material Goals

Short-Term Goal	Estimated Cost	Estimated Date
Take scuba lessons	$175	Now
Jennifer's orthodontics	$1,500	6 months
Reupholster Grandma's couch	$1,400	6 months
Cousin Jessie's wedding in Virginia	$1,800	3 months
Save $50 per month for the next 12 months	$600	Starting Now

Simply list your goals; don't prioritize them or even think about how you will pay for them right now. At this point stay focused on the list and approximate cost. Don't worry about why you want or need these things.

Let's move on now to phase 4.

Phase 4: Living with a Spending Plan

This section explains how to develop a spending plan, create new habits, deal with inevitable lapses from the spending plan, and maintain new healthy behaviors. If you do not feel confident working with the complexities involved in a spending plan, hire an accountant, a debt counselor, or a financial planner to help you to do the actual number crunching.

The spending plan is the primary tool for achieving your dreams and visions. It guides every dollar coming into your household. It is all-inclusive, realistic, and reflective of your unique lifestyle. A spending plan brings structure to chaotic, out-of-control spending. It shapes your spending into categories and reminds you that your paycheck is finite. It plans for everything: day-to-day expenses, repairs and replacements, long-term dreams and goals, and emergency funds.

A spending plan ensures that sufficient funds are available for every personal and household need. With this plan, specific amounts are assigned or allocated for each category. The spending plan helps you to determine if you are appropriately using your money.

Both deprivers and indulgers need to use the spending plan. Compulsive spenders practice containing spending to match the allocations. In contrast, deprivers learn to expand spending to fit each category allocation. If you are familiar with eating disorders, you'll note that the treatment process for money problems and money addiction is similar to that for food addicts; just as everyone needs to eat, everyone needs to manage money. An anorexic learns to eat *up* to the food plan; an overeater learns to eat *down* to the food plan. Similarly, a spending plan helps every addict achieve normalcy with money.

A spending plan allows you to see your expenses as concrete, black-and-white numbers. People with a problematic relationship with money are often not realistic about how many expenses one paycheck has to cover. You have to understand that a portion of today's paycheck has to pay for future expenses. A portion is needed when the rent or credit card bill comes due later in the month; another portion is set aside to pay for your vacation or the quarterly insurance premium in several months.

As you develop your spending plan, remember that all of your possessions will have to be replaced or repaired over time. The dishwasher will break; the brakes will go. This means that you need to think ahead to include a savings category for these repairs and replacements. You also need to anticipate that technology (computers and cell phones) becomes obsolete, so you must save for replacements. A spending plan helps you see that money from today's paycheck is needed to pay for expenses in the future, so you cannot spend your entire paycheck this week.

How a Spending Plan Differs from a Budget

We hear that budgets are necessary for financial well-being. A spending plan is similar to a budget, but it is more realistic. The problem with most budgets is that they are often inaccurate because they are not based on actual numbers. Often they're constructed by guessing or estimating expenses. Budgets are ineffective because you can use wishful thinking in budgets and make the numbers say what you want them to say. A spending plan, however, is based on your *actual* records of expenses. For instance, your grocery allocation is based on a month of actual grocery receipts, not what you would like to spend on groceries.

Your spending plan will deal with your annual expenses and allocate them on a monthly basis. We all have bills that are paid quarterly, semiannually, or annually (such as insurance or membership dues), as well as expenses that occur now and then, such as replacing a furnace or repairing the gutters. A spending plan helps you remember when these kinds of bills are due and shows you how to save for them every month.

The process is simple but a bit tedious. You are going to gather your expenses. Those that occur only once a year will be divided by 12 to get the monthly amount you need to set aside for that annual bill. Seasonal expenses (lawn care, snow removal) are handled in the same way as annual ones: divide the total figure for the year by 12. Those that occur weekly, such as therapy, newspapers, or music lessons, will be multiplied by 4.3 to arrive at the monthly expense for that item. No matter how frequent or infrequent the expense, there's a way to build it into your spending plan as an average monthly cost.

A cautionary note: Indulgers often have difficulty staying with a monthly plan and do better when they break their expenses down to weekly costs so they know when they are overspending. For example, if you consistently go beyond your monthly allotment for eating out, then break that down to a weekly allotment. In this example, an indulger might convert his monthly $43 allocation for dining out to $10 per week on dining out. So, each week, if your $10 is gone, you know you have spent your amount for that category.

How to Construct the Plan

The following six steps are essential for a successful plan:

1. Determine spending categories from your records.

2. Get acquainted with the Spending Plan Worksheet.

3. Determine the average monthly amount for each category.

4. Match total spending to income.

5. Balance the plan monthly.

6. Implement the spending plan.

Step 1. Determine Spending Categories from Your Records

Remember how in phase 2 you gathered your expense records and recorded your daily expenditures? While the goal of those activities was to help break through your denial and learn to accept and follow guidance, there's now another use for all that work—you can use those records to begin your spending plan.

Begin by flipping through those records. If they are on separate sheets, you can divide them into piles. Your spending categories will emerge as you look at your spending records. Typically, there are two types of categories, the *essentials* and the *wants*. The essentials include housing, utilities, transportation, food, clothing, health care, repairs, and taxes. Categories for the wants (nonessentials, lifestyle expenses, and so on) vary for each person but typically include expenses such as entertainment, gifts, charitable giving, hobby, and vacations. For example, if you have many hobbies, you need a category for hobbies, while someone else who doesn't have hobbies won't need that category. When creating your plan, give a category to every type of expense.

PEOPLE WITH MONEY PROBLEMS AND MONEY ADDICTIONS TYPICALLY CAN'T TELL THE DIFFERENCE BETWEEN ESSENTIAL *NEEDS* AND *WANTS*. SUCH PEOPLE ARE SAID TO WANT WHAT THEY WANT WHEN THEY WANT IT.

People with money problems and money addictions typically can't tell the difference between essential *needs* and *wants*. Such people are said to want what they want when they want it. If you are an indulger, that statement sums you up perfectly. You usually want a lot of stuff, and your faulty thinking leads you to believe that all these things you want are needs. You spend excessively on wants and neglect true needs, such as your monthly mortgage payment, car repair, medical care, or savings for your child's education. You sometimes spend a lot of money on little items, which leaves you no money for things you might really need. For instance, you might be spending so much on clothing that you can never save up enough money to replace your furnace.

If you are a depriver, on the other hand, you distortedly think that your needs or the necessities of life are something extra, or wants. Deprivers minimize essentials like appropriate dental care. Appropriate health and dental care is a need for every person at every income level, not a want. Because deprivers always try to "make do," they scale their life back to bare-bones necessities. Those deprivers who hoard money may also neglect needs in a different manner. For example, a hoarder may choose to live in a high-end neighborhood but disregard the landscape requirements of the neighborhood association.

Whether indulger or depriver, it's crucial that you know the difference between your needs and wants. In recovery, indulgers concentrate on reining in their definition of needs. The challenge for deprivers is to grow comfortable with their needs and practice expanding into their wants. It takes time to develop these skills. Be patient with yourself, as these changes won't come naturally.

To get started on changing your picture of needs and wants, think about some of the ways you have confused them. Every person has a different lifestyle and draws a different line between needs and wants. For everyone, food, shelter, transportation, clothing, and health care are basic survival needs. However, you may rationalize to yourself that you need a more expensive car for your job. In recovery, it's important to ask yourself why you believe that type of car is necessary. Differentiating needs from wants is problematic in the opposite direction also. One person might decide that dining out is not a need but a want, because you can save money by preparing your own food. But you can also argue that spending money to dine out accomplishes additional essential functions: it is a social outlet, provides a special reward to children, and reduces stress.

Because everyone has different life circumstances, no one but you can categorize your spending for you. It takes time to recognize the categories that best accommodate your life circumstances. Reflect on the list of categories in the sidebar "Types of Expenses and Income" (page 123) to see which you believe are needs and which are wants.

Types of Expenses and Income

EXPENSES

Shelter:
- Rent or Mortgage
- Property Taxes
- Property Insurance
- Heat
- Utilities
- Telephone
- Water
- Décor
- Replacements, Purchases
- Maintenance, Cleaning
- Garden Supplies
- Garbage Collection
- Association Fees

Transportation:
- Car Payments
- Insurance
- Gasoline
- Maintenance, Cleaning
- License
- Bus, Taxi, Tolls, Parking

Food:
- Groceries
- Delivered Goods, e.g., Pizza
- Snacks
- Work Lunches
- School Lunches

Clothing:
- Personal
- Spouse or Partner
- Children
- Maintenance, Cleaning

Entertainment:
- Vacations
- Meals Out
- Movies, Plays, Music
- Hobbies
- Spectator Sports
- Sports Equipment, Toys
- Electronic Equipment
- TV, Cable TV, Public TV

Savings:
- Credit Union, Bank
- Education
- Retirement
- Contingency

Health:
- Insurance
- Doctor
- Dentist
- Medications
- Therapy, Massage
- Exercise Classes, Equipment

Education:
- Lessons, Tuition
- Books, Papers, Magazines
- Supplies

Family:
- Life Insurance
- Legal
- Child Care: Daily
- Child Care: Occasional
- Allowances
- Gifts
- Holidays
- Pets: Food and Supplies
- Pets: Vet Care

Donations:
- House of Worship
- Political
- Charitable

Personal:
- Barber, Beauty Shop
- Toiletries
- Postage
- Alcohol
- Computer: Purchase, Repair
- Computer: Software, Supplies

Installment Payments:
- Credit Cards
- Department Store
- Student Loan
- Others

Miscellaneous:
- Union and Membership Dues
- Taxes: Social Security, Income (Federal, State, Local)
- Unreimbursed Business Expenses

INCOME

- Paycheck(s)
- Dividends
- Interest
- Social Security
- Pension
- Gifts

Step 2. Get Acquainted with the Spending Plan Worksheet
The Spending Plan Worksheet is used for three purposes: to track your monthly spending, to determine your monthly average spending and spending plan goal, and to balance the plan monthly. Chart 8-3 shows an abbreviated form of the worksheet, provided here to help you get familiar with it. A complete blank worksheet can be found in appendix C, or you may download the free reproducible journal that contains a copy of this worksheet. Visit hazelden.org/bookstore. On the *Spent* page, click on "reproducible journal with worksheets." Make copies of the worksheet before filling it in, as you will need one for each month.

Refer to chart 8-3 as you read the explanations that follow. The full worksheet in appendix C or in the journal will help you get a better feeling for all the categories and subcategories of expenses and income that you will need to track. (These same categories and subcategories are also shown in the sidebar "Types of Expenses and Income.")

- Columns 1 and 2, Category and Expense, show the major categories of expenses and income in your life.

- Columns 3 to 6, Cash, Checkbook, Credit Card 1, and Credit Card 2, are the sources for recording your spending. You pay for some things with cash, some via check, and some via credit card. You'll be entering the amounts from those various sources in these columns.

- Column 7 is the total spending for each category/expense.

- Column 8, Spending Plan Goal, is where you will enter the amounts you want to be achieving. The amounts in this column will be determined in step 4.

- In column 9, Difference, you will compare (each month) the difference between your planned goals and your actual expenditures. This figure will be determined in step 5.

As you fill in this chart in subsequent steps, you can either use the actual records that you have been keeping since chapter 7 (phase 2), or you can use previous spending records. If you choose to use your previous records, then gather together old checkbook registers, credit card statements, and bank statements. You can estimate your cash spending based on how much cash you

CHART 8-3

Abbreviated Spending Plan Worksheet

Month _____

❶	❷ Expense	❸ Cash	❹ Checkbook	❺ Credit Card 1	❻ Credit Card 2	❼ Total	❽ Spending Plan Goal	❾ Difference
Shelter	Rent or Mortgage							
Transportation	Car Payment 1							
Food	Groceries							
Clothing	Personal							
Entertainment	Vacations							
Savings (DEPOSITS INTO ACCOUNTS)	Credit Union, Bank							
Health	Insurance							
Education	Lessons, Tuition							
Family	Life Insurance							
Donations	House of Worship							
Personal	Barber, Beauty Shop							
Installment Payments	Credit Card 1							
Miscellaneous	Union and Membership Dues							
TOTAL OUTGO								

Income	Amount
Paycheck 1	
TOTAL INCOME	

have taken out of the bank and then apply it toward the things you typically spend cash for, such as babysitters, cigarettes, gasoline, lunches, tips, and so on.

For each expense that applies to you, fill in the columns Cash, Checkbook, Credit Card 1, and Credit Card 2 with the amounts you have spent. (If you need to add rows for more credit or debit cards, recreate the worksheet in a spreadsheet or cut it apart and add a new column.)

So, for example, let's say for clothing for yourself you've spent $20 in cash, $126 from your checkbook, $78 on credit card 1, and $0 on credit card 2. You insert those figures in their appropriate spaces and then add them together to get a total of $224.

Repeat this process for each area for which you have expenditures. And don't forget to include major expenses from the previous year, such as annual property taxes, seasonal expenses, and any large purchases or repairs.

Some expenses are easy because they are fixed each month (car payment, rent, installment loan payment, and perhaps utility bill). For these easy categories, you know that your spending plan allocation is the same every month, so that's your amount.

In other categories, you may make a payment only twice a year, such as with property tax. Take the total yearly amount and divide it by 12. So if you make two payments of $1,800 each for property tax, your average monthly expense is $3,600 ($1,800 + $1,800) divided by 12, or $300 a month.

In cases where the expenses are infrequent, you may need to get creative. If you know you spent $2,200 last year in auto repairs but only $200 this year, you can take the total ($2,400) and divide it by 24 months, for an average monthly expenditure of $100.

Don't worry if every category is not covered, and don't seek perfection. Just start to fill in one worksheet every month.

The process of looking at your prior check registers and credit card statements arouses many emotions. As you chronicle your purchases, you'll probably be surprised to see realistic figures about your spending. You might feel shame as you witness the mess you've made through overindulgence or deprivation. You might be angry with yourself or fearful as you see the seriousness of your situation. Or you might feel relieved and hopeful to finally take stock of the situation. However you react, keep filling out the worksheet, because the Spending Plan Worksheet will show you why you are so pinched financially.

This step takes time, but it will help you get a very clear grasp of your current monthly costs. You can look at this as an outside limit; if you've been indulging, you will need to find ways to reduce those costs. In order for the spending plan to work, you can't go over that limit.

Once you've done this for every category, add up all your categories to arrive at your total monthly spending. Also include minimum payments on all your debts.

You will note that you have not yet filled in the columns labeled "Spending Plan Goal" and "Difference." That is the subject of our next two steps.

Chart 8-4a shows part of the Spending Plan Worksheet filled in for a sample month.

Step 3. Determine the Average Monthly Amount for Each Category

Now that you've gathered your records and familiarized yourself with the Spending Plan Worksheet, you now need to determine your average monthly spending in each expense area. If you are comfortable with math and numbers, this will be fairly easy. If you are not, seek the help of a trusted friend, an accountant, or a financial planner.

Using the Six-Month Worksheet, transfer your totals for each month to its corresponding cell. In the column labeled "Number of Months Entered," put the number of months that you are working with. Divide the total for each expense by the number of months entered to arrive at your monthly average. (Put these amounts in the column marked "Monthly Average.") Chart 8-4b is a sample showing six months added and then divided to arrive at the average monthly spending for each category. A blank version of the full worksheet can be found in appendix C and in the journal.

CHART 8-4a

Sample Monthly Figures

This chart shows expenses in the categories of food, clothing, entertainment, and savings for the month of January.

Month _____ January _____

Expense	Cash	Checkbook	Credit Card 1	Credit Card 2	Total	Spending Plan Goal	Difference
Food							
Groceries	164	143	52		359		
Delivered Goods, e.g., Pizza	42				42		
Snacks	18				18		
Work Lunches	9		42		51		
School Lunches		60			60		
Clothing							
Personal	22		53		75		
Spouse or Partner				68	68		
Children	14	35		51	100		
Maintenance, Cleaning	24	11			35		
Entertainment							
Vacations	70	205			275		
Meals Out	147	16			163		
Movies, Plays, Music			47		47		
Hobbies		36			36		
Spectator Sports							
Sports Equipment, Toys	42	5			47		
Electronic Equipment							
TV, Cable TV, Public TV		35			35		
Savings (DEPOSITS INTO ACCOUNTS)							
Credit Union, Bank	150	150			150		
Education	100	100			100		
Retirement	200	200			200		
Contingency	25	25			25		

CHART 8-4b

Averages of Six Months of Sample Monthly Expenses

This chart shows total monthly expenses for six months in the same categories, the total, and the average monthly expenses. A blank version of this worksheet can be found in appendix C and in the journal.

Expense	January	February	March	April	May	June	Total	# of Months Entered	Monthly Average
Food									
Groceries	359	402	375	299	450	320	2,205	6	367.50
Delivered Goods, e.g., Pizza	42	14	35	14	7	29	141	6	23.50
Snacks	18	10	7	13	9	4	61	6	10.17
Work Lunches	51	43	10	42	17	27	190	6	31.67
School Lunches	60	48	60	60	48	30	306	6	51.00
Clothing									
Personal	75	13	40	0	350	0	478	6	79.67
Spouse or Partner	68	0	0	17	120	0	205	6	34.17
Children	100	74	0	118	84	21	397	6	66.17
Maintenance, Cleaning	35	15	0	22	0	10	82	6	13.67
Entertainment									
Vacations	275	275	275	275	275	275	1,650	6	275.00
Meals Out	163	98	175	114	125	114	789	6	131.50
Movies, Plays, Music	47	0	119	0	0	0	166	6	27.67
Hobbies	36	14	22	7	49	0	128	6	21.33
Spectator Sports	0	0	0	0	0	0	0	6	0
Sports Equipment, Toys	47	0	22	124	0	0	193	6	32.17
Electronic Equipment	0	0	0	0	0	0	0	6	0
TV, Cable TV, Public TV	35	35	35	35	35	35	210	6	35.00
Savings (DEPOSITS INTO ACCOUNTS)									
Credit Union, Bank	150	100	100	100	100	100	650	6	108.33
Education	100	90	90	90	90	90	550	6	91.67
Retirement	200	190	190	170	190	170	1,110	6	185.00
Contingency	25	25	15	15	20	10	110	6	18.33

Step 4. Match Total Spending to Income

Tracking and calculating your current monthly average spending is a great start. Next, your total spending must match your actual income. In chapter 4 we learned that the only type of problem money user who does not struggle with debt is the hoarder. The remaining types of problem users are in debt because their average spending has probably exceeded their income and they've been relying on credit to pay bills. *If you are going to stop living on credit, your total expenditures can't exceed your income.*

Once you have calculated your monthly spending averages, total all of them up and see how they compare with your income. You will probably see a big difference. See if you can make reductions in the categories to make your spending more in line with your income. A special worksheet, the Shaving Worksheet, can help with this. A sample is shown in chart 8-5, and there's a blank copy in appendix C and in the journal.

When you don't earn enough to cover your spending, you have two choices: spend less or earn more income. Sometimes increasing your income is the simpler solution. So get together with your friends, family, therapist, or other support systems to brainstorm ideas about how to earn more. You can earn more by changing to a better-paying job, working more overtime hours, or taking on an additional part-time job. You can also turn hobbies into income-producing opportunities.

 WHEN YOU DON'T EARN ENOUGH TO COVER YOUR SPENDING, YOU HAVE TWO CHOICES: SPEND LESS OR EARN MORE INCOME.

You can also sell possessions, though this is a short-term solution because eventually you'll run out of objects to sell. Nevertheless, selling possessions will give you some extra cash as you think about how to make larger, more serious changes.

If you can't increase your income, then you'll have to spend less. To spend less, you'll have to shave or pare down your monthly allocations. Go down the list, category by category, and reduce any category that you can by a realistic amount. You must realistically discern between needs and wants.

CHART 8-5

Sample Shaving Worksheet

In this partial chart, you can see how we adjusted expenses to bring them more in line with goals. (Numbers in the "Monthly Average" column from chart 8-4b were rounded and inserted into column A below.) For example, money was saved on pizza, work lunches, clothing, and so forth. A blank version of the full worksheet can be found in appendix C and in the journal.

Expense	A Six-Month Spending Average	B Adjustment (Reduction in Plan)	C New Spending Plan
Food			
Groceries	368	0	368
Delivered Goods, e.g., Pizza	24	-5	19
Snacks	10	0	10
Work Lunches	32	-10	22
School Lunches	51	0	51
Clothing			
Personal	80	-30	50
Spouse or Partner	34	-5	29
Children	66	0	66
Maintenance, Cleaning	14	-3	11
Entertainment			
Vacations	275	-35	240
Meals Out	132	-40	92
Movies, Plays, Music	28	-5	23
Hobbies	21	-4	17
Spectator Sports	0	0	0
Sports Equipment, Toys	32	-5	27
Electronic Equipment	0	0	0
TV, Cable TV, Public TV	35	0	35
Savings (DEPOSITS INTO ACCOUNTS)			
Credit Union, Bank	108	-75	33
Education	92	-10	82
Retirement	185	-20	165
Contingency	18	2	20

At this time, for most of my clients—and probably for you—it becomes very clear that many categories cannot be reduced. Your mortgage and car payments are fixed, and others such as utilities, insurances, and even groceries probably can't be reduced by much. Keep at it; continue examining each category individually to see if you can cut back until you have sufficiently trimmed it down to match your income.

Remember, you are reading this book because you have been spending more than your income. *Do not fret; there's still hope.* Ask your financial helpmate to give you an extra set of eyes on your situation. Brainstorm with others about how they have reduced expenses. (Just a reminder: these circumstances usually don't apply to hoarders.)

Here are some ground rules for setting goals in your category allocations and for paring back in certain categories.

1. Do not pare back categories for repairs and maintenance of mechanical items, automobiles, and your home. When faced with unexpected events, people with money problems impulsively turn to credit cards. When things break down, you feel panicked and victimized and tend to create more chaos. You must avoid this. Preparing for repairs helps you eliminate financial crisis and trust that the spending plan will take care of basic needs. When you have saved specifically for repairs, there won't be a crisis.

2. Include a category for general savings, either savings for retirement or contingency savings to accumulate three to six months of living expenses. You can begin small, with $1 per week or $10 per month savings habit. Keep it simple—a piggy bank, coffee can, envelope, or special bank account. People with money problems must develop a regular savings habit.

3. Do not eliminate items or experiences that are a part of your vision for your future. It's better to keep a token amount like $1 per month in a category than to cut it out entirely. This will offset feelings of deprivation, particularly if you are making drastic cuts. Remember you need to trim because you are in debt and want to be free of debt. Your old habits have caused hardship. Continuing your old behaviors will only generate more pain. As you grow with the plan and align your

income and expenditures, you will have an opportunity to increase your contribution to your vision.

4. Include replacements or purchases for the next year. Your spending plan must be realistic, workable, and reflect your current *and* future needs. Create a list, like the one in chart 8-2 on page 118, of what you'll need to purchase or replace in the next year, and put those categories into the spending plan. This enables you to begin monthly saving toward future needs.

5. Also think about any previous financial obligations and commitments and account for these upcoming purchases in the spending plan. (Refer to the list of long-term goals you made earlier in this chapter.) If a spending plan is constructed and these things aren't accounted for, you'll tend to believe there is excess money when in fact the totality of future spending hasn't been accounted for. Indulgers usually spend money even before it comes in. You probably have grandiose ideas about what you can afford. It's not unusual for me to hear, "Oh, by the way, I'm going to Paris; we've had this trip planned for a year. It really won't cost that much because we're staying with friends." Or, "Oh, by the way, I signed up for a health club for another $60 a month." People with money problems don't recognize that these commitments involve finances, so they do not plan how to get the money for these additional purchases.

6. Include minimum debt payments. Permanent debt liberation is your ultimate goal. Debts are not bills—they *will* go away completely one day if you live without credit cards. If you truly commit to a life free of incurring more debt, you will not have more debt. This means that all of your debt is an old expense that will be eliminated. So the focus of a spending plan is to learn how to be normal with money, how to spend appropriately, and how to take care of your needs so you won't need credit cards and other debt tools.

Think of people you know who have gained and lost the same weight many times over the years. If they'd only learn to eat right, you think, they'd be okay. We use that approach with money. The more you focus on life in a spending plan, the more your true needs will be covered and your credit card lifestyle will recede into the background.

Keeping these guidelines in mind will help you tune up your plan. If you are an indulger, now is the time to think again about *needs* versus *wants*. Are the clothes you are purchasing truly a need or just something you want? Where else can you trim back to bring your plan into better alignment?

After you've made adjustments to your categories/expenses in the Shaving Worksheet, you'll come up with new spending plan amounts (in column C). Transfer the numbers in this column to column 8, Spending Plan Goal, in the Spending Plan Worksheet. Make new copies of the blank Spending Plan Worksheet, then add the spending plan goals. (You'll need a copy of the worksheet for each future month.) Your Spending Plan Goal column will remain consistent until you make a new spending plan.

Step 5. Balance the Plan Monthly

After a few months of living with your spending plan and recording your spending, look at each category and compare the actual spending with your spending plan goal. Write this down in the last column on the spending plan labeled "Difference."

Which categories cause you trouble? Do you overspend or underspend in the same categories each month? If you consistently overspend, then increase the spending plan allocation for that category, but be sure to decrease another category by the same amount. Look over the Difference column to see where you are unable to keep to the plan. What do you need to adjust? Ask your financial helpmate to point out patterns. Get help from your support network to keep to the plan.

Life is fluid; everyone's life circumstances change, and your spending plan will change to accommodate changes. New expenses emerge; others are no longer needed. Child care may be removed, but children's lessons will increase. Debt gets paid off. You get married and living expenses lessen with a spouse to share in them. At times, your plan will include weddings, college, and major home renovations. Your clothing allowance goes down when you retire. There will always be fluctuations to your plan, so you should reassess it monthly at first, and once per year after you have built your savings.

Chart 8-6, on page 136, shows the same example we've been looking at, comparing the person's goals with actual expenses.

HOW TO REPAY YOUR DEBTS

Most people with money problems have significant debt burdens. Traditional financial planners will recommend two approaches to repaying debt: (1) Pay the creditors as much as you can, as fast as you can; or (2) Liquidate your assets to pay off debts.

Both of these work, but they are not suited for indulgers, whether they are problem users or full-blown money addicts. Indulgers have continuous "leaks" in their budget. Unless you have plugged up your spending leaks, you will just rack up more debt once you pay it off. Or, like a binge dieter, when you deprive yourself in order to pay off debts, you will probably go on a spending spree after the debts are paid off. Furthermore, if you succeed at the rapid payoff, it will reduce your experience of negative consequences *before you have learned to handle cash and follow a spending plan.* As an indulger, it is more important that you learn to follow the plan than to rapidly pay off debt.

**Your first goal is to learn to use a spending plan;
paying off your debts is your second goal.**

This approach is slow and gradual; it doesn't take the evidence of your money problems away. You learn to balance many expenses while you are paying off debt. After the debt is eliminated, you already know how to live within a spending plan—so you won't feel the need to go crazy with spending, like a binge dieter who, after hitting goal weight, then raids the local bakery.

You can do this by devoting your payments to the high interest cards or smallest balances first. As you retire debts, you take the payment amounts and apply them to the next largest one until they are all gone. Or you can pay equal amounts to all creditors at the same time, paying them in proportion to the total debt. Here are the steps:

1. Talk to your creditors: be proactive and call them before they call you. Ask for a supervisor if you are not treated respectfully.

2. Don't promise any payment unless you are certain to keep the promise: you will have more leverage with them if you are consistent and keep to your promises.

3. Don't let them bully you, scare you, or shame you about your circumstances.

4. If you keep your commitments, you will earn the company's respect, but more important, your own self-respect will return.

5. Arrange for lower interest rates. Be persistent. Keep asking.

Month _____

CHART 8-6

Sample of the Spending Plan Worksheet with Goals and Actual Amounts Filled In

Expense	Cash	Checkbook	Credit Card 1	Credit Card 2	Actual Total	Spending Plan Goal	Difference
Food							
Groceries	164	143	52		359	368	9
Delivered Goods, e.g., Pizza	42				42	19	-23
Snacks	18				18	10	-8
Work Lunches	9		42		51	22	-29
School Lunches		60			60	51	-9
Clothing							
Personal	22		53		75	50	-25
Spouse or Partner				68	68	29	-39
Children	14	35		51	100	66	-34
Maintenance, Cleaning	24	11			35	11	-24
Entertainment							
Vacations	70	205			275	240	-35
Meals Out	147	16			163	92	-71
Movies, Plays, Music			47		47	23	-24
Hobbies		36			36	17	-19
Spectator Sports					0	0	0
Sports Equipment, Toys	42	5			47	27	-20
Electronic Equipment					0	0	0
TV, Cable TV, Public TV		35			35	35	0
Savings (DEPOSITS INTO ACCOUNTS)							
Credit Union, Bank		150			150	33	-117
Education		100			100	82	-18
Retirement		200			200	165	-35
Contingency		25			25	20	-5

Step 6. Implement the Spending Plan

The first problem you'll have in working with a spending plan is very tight cash flow. *Cash flow* is different from the *spending plan*. The spending plan is a plan on paper. *Cash flow* is the money you have in your wallet or checking account. Cash flow refers to how much money (cash) is coming into your checking account and where it is being spent. Expect your cash flow to be tight at the beginning, because you are now using cash (either actual cash or funds available in your checking account) to pay for items that were previously paid for with credit. The elastic or limitless feeling is gone. To make things even tighter, your new life without credit cards requires you to tie up cash in savings. This pinch is normal.

To implement the plan at first, buy only absolute necessities—rent, utilities, transportation, and food. Avoid all other spending, and do not use credit cards to prop yourself up. Don't worry; you'll have lots of opportunities in the future to make purchases. For now, focus on the basics. If you stay within your limits and the plan matches your true income, eventually extra cash will free up. You can make decisions about purchasing extra items when you have more cash.

You also need to determine how much actual cash you should carry with you. Some people simply cannot handle any cash in their wallet without spending it immediately. Others need to carry cash in order to practice keeping it without acting on urges to spend it. This is an individual choice; you will want to experiment until you develop greater consciousness about your financial choices. Make a list showing which items you normally pay cash for and which ones you pay for by check, to determine a reasonable amount of cash to carry on a weekly basis. For instance, if you normally buy groceries and gas with cash, then take that allocation out of your paycheck and carry only that amount with you each week.

You might feel panicked and unsure about how to manage the situation without the elasticity of credit. Hang in there; it will get easier. Try experimenting with the following techniques to help you during the tight cash flow.

CALENDAR SYSTEM

Get a monthly calendar and mark the calendar with your paycheck date along with any expenses due that month. This is like a spreadsheet that visually reminds you what bills are due. Look at your paycheck on the calendar to see

CHART 8-7

Calendar System of Income and Expenses

Sunday	Monday	Tuesday	Wednesday	Thursday	Friday	Saturday
			1 Mortgage $657	2 Timmy's lesson $30	3 **Paycheck $900**	4
5	6 Visa paydown $18	7 Macy's paydown $23	8	9 Timmy's lesson $30	10	11
12	13	14	15 Insurance $227	16 Timmy's lesson $30	17 **Paycheck $900**	18
19	20 Utilities $169	21 Discover paydown $33	22 Phone $38.99	23 Timmy's lesson $30	24	25
26	27	28	29	30 Timmy's lesson $30	31 **Paycheck $900**	

in advance how it will be divided up. Chart 8-7 provides a partial example.

You can also be accountable to another person about which bills you will pay with each paycheck. This accountability ensures that your needs will be covered.

You can use a twelve-month calendar to help you predict expenses ahead of time. Another version of this calendar system is the Weekly Income and Expense Tracker. A blank version of this is provided in appendix C, "Weekly Income and Expense Tracker" (page 215) and in the reproducible journal. You'll find instructions for its use there.

ENVELOPE SYSTEM

As an experiment to raise your consciousness, try the old-fashioned envelope system. When you receive your paycheck, convert it into five-, ten-, and twenty-dollar bills. Then write the monthly allocation amount on envelopes labeled with your spending plan categories and place that amount of money into it. When the cash for clothing is gone for the month, then you know you cannot buy more clothing until the next month. Even though it's cumbersome and time-consuming, this system teaches concrete, basic cash management. Just try it for one or two months and see what happens. You might use this cash-in-envelope system only for categories where you consistently overspend. For instance, a person who overspends on dining out may need to use the cash envelope system solely for that category.

IRREGULAR EXPENDITURES

Some expenses come due seasonally or once or twice a year, such as home insurance, lawn maintenance, and tuition payments. These expenses are predictable and relatively fixed. Using an envelope system or actually opening a bank account specifically for these expenses helps to predict and save toward them.

FLUCTUATING EXPENSES

Some categories vary greatly over time. Examples are vacations, car repair, and home improvement. One month you have a $700 car repair and then no other large repairs for seven months. When you start using a spending plan, $700 might not be available (without borrowing or using credit cards) for that category. To solve the cash flow pinch, you may need to "borrow" against another category and use the other category's allocation to pay for the car repair. Next month, replace the money in the category you borrowed from.

Before your recovery journey, these unexpected repairs were your excuse to use credit cards. The spending plan enables you to juggle things until your cash flow situation eases up.

Another method to handle fluctuating expenses is to open a checking or savings account particularly for one specific category. This is reminiscent of old-fashioned Christmas Club accounts, into which a person deposited money all year long and withdrew it at the end of the year for Christmas expenses. For example, if you always have difficulty saving for a vacation, you could open a bank account and deposit a monthly allocation in it, and not touch that money until you are ready to take your vacation.

You can also group several categories together and make deposits into one bank account for these categories. For example, chart 8-8, on the next page, shows four fluctuating expenses that could be grouped together into one bank account. This person would deposit $320 ($100 + $95 + $50 + $75) monthly into this account. All money accumulated in this account is strictly earmarked for these particular fluctuating expenses.

Summary of Spending Plan

A spending plan takes every single expense into account. This prevents financial chaos, because financial needs are handled with foresight and common sense. Using your spending plan lets you experience bill paying as a regular, planned event. Money comes into your life through its various channels. You use some of this money to maintain your daily functions, and you store some for future use.

A spending plan teaches you the finite boundaries of money and what you can afford according to basic laws of mathematics. You need these boundaries because your troubled relationship with money causes you to bend reality and pretend that you don't need to live by the same rules that everyone else does. The spending plan helps you to make decisions about whether something is an appropriate purchase for you or not. It becomes your yardstick and ensures that your spending is preplanned, calculated, and limited. By working with finances in this manner, your recovery becomes clear-cut. If you veer from your plan and overspend in a category, it's clear as daylight that you have fallen off your plan. And you know what will happen—a return to the painful consequences of problem money use or full-blown addiction.

A spending plan is not a prison or a cage. It simply gives limits for those who don't know how to live within their income. Think of your spending plan

CHART 8-8

Fluctuating Expenses

Travel				
Annual: $1,200.00				
	Deposit	Expense	Purchase	Balance
January	$100			$100
February	$100			$200
March	$100			$300
April	$100	$400	Trav. City	$0
May	$100			$100
June	$100			$200
July	$100			$300
August	$100			$400
September	$100			$500
October	$100			$600
November	$100			$700
December	$100	$700	Maine	$100

House Repairs				
Annual: $1,140.00				
	Deposit	Expense	Purchase	Balance
January	$95	$75	plumber	$20
February	$95			$115
March	$95	$356	water heater	-$146
April	$95	$45	gutters	-$96
May	$95			-$1
June	$95	$450	paint	-$356
July	$95			-$261
August	$95			-$166
September	$95	$75	furnace inspection	-$146
October	$95			-$51
November	$95			$44
December	$95			$139

Clothing				
Annual: $600.00				
	Deposit	Expense	Purchase	Balance
January	$50	$25.62	boots	$24.38
February	$50	$156.47	winter coat	-$82.09
March	$50			-$32.09
April	$50	$15.00	underwear	$2.91
May	$50	$274.14	summer clothes	-$221.23
June	$50			-$171.23
July	$50			-$121.23
August	$50			-$71.23
September	$50	$45.49	blouse	-$66.72
October	$50	$64.37	shoes	-$81.09
November	$50			-$31.09
December	$50			$18.91

Car Repairs				
Annual: $900.00				
	Deposit	Expense	Purchase	Balance
January	$75	$25	oil chg.	$50
February	$75			$125
March	$75			$200
April	$75	$25	oil chg.	$250
May	$75	$200	tires	$125
June	$75	$25	brakes checked	$175
July	$75			$250
August	$75	$25	oil chg.	$300
September	$75			$375
October	$75	$250	muffler	$200
November	$75			$275
December	$75	$25	oil chg.	$325

as a magic carpet. Step off the flying carpet, and you'll fall to the ground. Stay on the carpet, and it will take you to places not currently possible. Best of all, it's a carpet you've woven from your dreams for the future and your hard work in the present. That is the promise and gift of recovery.

Learning to Make Healthy Spending Choices

Learning to follow your plan involves learning to make healthy spending choices. For you, that means being sure that the plan you've made reflects your goals, values, and commitments, and that the choices you make fit your plan. If they fit your plan, then by definition they reflect the goals and values you have—as well as the commitments you've made to pay off debts, support your children's growth, and other commitments.

Every person has his or her own individual patterns of spending that bring pleasure. These patterns are as unique as a fingerprint. One person spends money on designer cigars, another to maintain a classic car, another on travel to reenact the Civil War, another giving to charity. The choices are yours to make, and the consequences are yours to suffer or enjoy, depending on the choice.

A spending plan will help you be happy with your choices. You'll be more successful if your spending choices align with your values, because you'll receive more pleasure from your money. This pleasure grows and gives positive reinforcement to continue with further positive, life-affirming choices.

Most people with money problems have little experience making truly healthy spending choices. So you will need criteria for making spending decisions. Here are some ways to think about your spending so that you learn to make healthy choices:

- If a specific purchase is important, then dedicate some time to figuring out how you will get the money to pay for it. What are you willing to give up so the numbers work for you? If you aren't willing to give anything up, perhaps the purchase is not as important to you as you thought.

- When you really want something, ask yourself how it fits with your other values and goals. Will purchasing it conflict with your values or express them? Will purchasing it bring you closer to your most important goals or move you further from them? Will purchasing it cause you to damage an important commitment to a spouse, partner, child, or friend?

- How much time and work will it require for you to pay for that item? Is that what you want to do?

- If you can't make the numbers work to make your purchase, are you willing to cut spending somewhere else or increase your income to get it?

- If there is something you really want, be sure you have a category to begin saving for it. Don't pretend you don't want these items and then go buy them anyway. Save for them. When faced with a choice, is the item something that you've really wanted and have saved for, or is it a whim?

- Is your interest in the thing you want to purchase the result of a passionate interest or an obsessive overindulgence? If unique hobbies or interests escalate and are pursued without a plan or in secrecy, then you want to see if the line has been crossed into money problems or full-blown money addiction.

When considering placing limits on your spending, you may feel defensive and think this book is just like your punitive father or depriving mother. This is because you have mistakenly believed that financial boundaries and limitations prevented you from having what you want. A spending plan will help you understand that's not the case. When choices come up in life, you look at your spending plan to determine if the purchase is appropriate for you. The plan is your yardstick, expressing limits and choices that you yourself set during a time of quiet thinking, not in the rush of a special offer. What seems like a choice may not be one at all, because choosing to spend on that item would put pressure on your bills somewhere else.

Banking Guidelines

The following guidelines will help you gain control of your finances and reduce the risk of impulsive purchases. (Note: These guidelines are for everyone but hoarders, who are likely already spending too much time thinking about banking.)

General Tips

Your accountant or financial planner has probably given you suggestions about banking. If not, the following list provides sensible ways to save money.

- Shop for low rates on checking account fees.
- Shop for high interest yields on savings accounts.

- Avoid bank penalties.
- Avoid ATM machine use.
- Develop regular banking habits; visit the bank only once per week.
- Balance your checkbook regularly, at least every month.

Checkbook Management

Try out several of the following strategies to balance your checkbook until you find one that works for you. Staying on top of your bank balance is a crucial step in recovery.

- Ask a friend, partner, or the bank to help you balance your checkbook.
- Hire a bookkeeper, accountant, or accounting student to do it for you.
- Check your balance regularly—either online, in person, or via the computerized telephone banking system.
- Highlight reconciled checks with a fluorescent pen in the checkbook register so you can see which checks are still outstanding.
- Some people find addition simpler than subtraction. If you're one of them, add up the checks you've written in your checkbook register. When all the checks you've written add up to your deposit amount, you can't write any more checks until you deposit more money.
- Round off the numbers when you record your checks, so that you only concern yourself with whole dollar amounts. This at least gives you an approximate balance for your checkbook.

There is a mathematical learning disorder, dyscalculia, which results in extensive mental strain to carry out even simple arithmetic tasks. If you suspect that you might have this, seek professional evaluation.

Bill Paying

You'll need to develop routines for paying your bills. Here are some suggestions to make bill paying easier:

- Set up automatic bill payments on everything you can. Set up automatic deposits for savings.
- Assign one regular spot in the house to store bills until they are due. Pay them from this same spot.

- Establish a regular time each week to pay bills.
- Record all regular bills into the checkbook register at the beginning of the month to help remember that bills are coming due.
- Utilize a bill payment calendar and schedule to pay bills.
- Address envelopes in advance to pay your bills.
- Get a bill-paying buddy and do it together.
- Go to a quiet, relaxing environment like the library or a coffee shop.

Developing Savings

The ability to save money demonstrates that impulsive spending is getting under control. As you gain the self-discipline to delay gratification, your self-worth improves.

You'll need different types of savings for different purposes.

Each week, you'll save for short-term expenses such as the rent, installments on a child's violin lessons, or getting a haircut. Each year, there are midterm expenses, such as a vacation, holiday gifts, or an annual furnace cleaning. Every three to five years, there are mid- to long-term expenses, such as home and car maintenance, illness, or a special celebration. Long-term savings, more than five years, are also needed for retirement, children's college education, a dream vacation, or a major home renovation or purchase.

Start saving immediately. It is somewhat of a spiritual and psychological exercise as you begin to leave money alone without touching it. Every start is worthwhile; five dollars a week is the perfect amount if that's what you can afford now. Make it convenient—a piggy bank, an automatic deduction from your paycheck, an envelope under your mattress. Make it fun; save coins to start with and see if you can keep those around without spending them. Next, add more coins to the beginning amount to see how you feel as you allow it to build without touching it. Then try saving one-dollar bills. Get a special envelope to hold all the money you save from forgoing your cappuccinos. However humble the start, take the step. Don't fret about what you haven't done in the past; start now. If you're ashamed or embarrassed of the savings you haven't done, just start now anyway. Whatever method you choose, do it regularly so it becomes a habit.

At first, when cash flow is tight, you may have to *occasionally* dip into savings. This might feel like two steps forward and one step back. However, if you can't eventually gain consistent momentum for savings to grow, you may be lapsing back into problem money use or addiction. Savings are for saving. This money is not for spending. If you use your savings for anything other than for what it was allocated, then you should consider whether you have relapsed.

Having a savings account alleviates your fear of unknown expenses cropping up. When you know you have the money to handle whatever comes up, you can focus on more rewarding aspects of life. Having money in the bank also makes you money via compound interest.

Lucy, a self-employed florist, is an example of a client who learned to save money. When she first sought help, she had a sizable credit card debt due to a business venture that never succeeded. She had no savings and felt ashamed that she had no retirement savings. She berated herself because she believed that every American could save $2,000 in an IRA account each year. At the time, she felt helpless to begin any type of savings and uneducated about how to invest retirement savings. With the coaching of her therapist, she opened an IRA and began to save $200 per year in a bank account. After two years, she was able to save $400 per year, and then doubled that to $800 per year until she was able to meet her goal of $2,000 in an IRA annually. At last report, Lucy had amassed about $74,000 in her retirement accounts and states that she feels good about "keeping some of the money she works hard for."

Summary

In this chapter, you've made substantial progress toward recovery from money problems and money addiction. You've created a life vision for yourself, setting a sense of where you want to go. You've developed personal and financial goals that accompany that vision. And you've worked out a way to turn that vision into a reality by creating a detailed spending plan. This plan is the ticket to your future; it is also the pathway out of the deeply troubled relationship with money that you've had. Writing the plan was hard, and sticking with it is even tougher.

In the next chapter, you will learn techniques to deal with the thoughts, feelings, and impulsive actions that can lead you away from your plan and back into money problems. This is hard work, but it will pay off for you.

• • •

Phase 5: Changing Your Thinking, Feelings, and Impulsive Actions

You now understand phase 4 of recovery. During that phase, you learned how to develop a spending plan both as a financial tool and as an expression of how you want to live your life in accordance with your values and dreams.

Your spending plan is a powerful tool, perhaps the most powerful you've wielded. But having the tool is not enough to conquer your dysfunctional financial behaviors. In this chapter, you will fully explore phase 5. You will learn to recognize situations, people, thoughts, feelings, and impulsive behaviors that can lead you back to your troubled relationship with money. You'll also learn about how to deal with relapse.

Triggers

Impulsive and addictive behavior is often catalyzed by what is called a *trigger*. A trigger is an experience that upsets you and activates your desire to act out. Triggers are unconscious. Sometimes triggers come from inside us, and sometimes they come from external circumstances that are beyond our control. Regardless of the source, you must learn to identify them so that you can make a plan to handle them constructively. This book classifies triggers according to whether they stem from external circumstances or internal thoughts and feelings.

External Triggers

External triggers are environmental circumstances that influence your money behaviors. Here is a list of external triggers:

1. Being at or exposed to *shopping outlets:*
   - A certain store
   - A certain mall
   - A special catalog
   - Web sites, such as eBay
   - Estate or garage sales

2. Being with or around *particular people:*
   - Your family (spouse or partner, child, sibling, parent)
   - People you feel envious of or compare yourself with
   - Certain people you shop with

3. Specific *events* or *times of year:*
   - Holidays
   - Seasons
   - Celebrations (birthdays, anniversaries, and so on)
   - Life transitions
   - Vacation
   - Beginning of school year

4. Specific *circumstances*
   - Sales at certain stores
   - Circulars, coupons, or special offers, such as 10 percent off a purchase if you open a charge card
   - Commercials on TV
   - Telemarketing calls
   - Release of a new product
   - Someone else getting something you want

In your notebook or in the space provided in the journal, list external triggers that are difficult for you.

To combat external triggers, you'll have to avoid these situations at first. Do not use the Internet for personal use for a certain amount of time. Call catalog companies and tell them to remove you from their mailing list. Make a spending plan just for your holiday season or for vacations.

In your notebook or journal, list other methods that you'll use to handle these triggers.

Internal Triggers

Internal triggers are numerous, more difficult to identify, and more difficult to avoid than external triggers. The two major categories of internal triggers are difficult feelings and distorted thinking. We'll start with some of the feelings that typically trigger a return to money problems, along with strategies for coping with them.

DIFFICULT FEELINGS

Difficult moods and feelings can trigger indulging or depriving behavior. Common triggers are listed here:

- Anger
- Anxiety or panic
- Depression
- Loss or grief
- Shame
- Boredom
- Pain
- Happiness

Think about this list and identify which feelings are difficult for you. If you don't know what feelings are triggers for you, then consider joining a support group or counseling with the specific goal of learning to identify your feelings.

You've been coping with your feelings already, whether you know it or not; your coping mechanism has been to indulge or deprive yourself. When you stop using money to handle your feelings, you'll need an entirely new repertoire of coping techniques: some to give you a sense of order when you're overwhelmed, some to stimulate you when you're bored, some to pep you up when you're depressed, and still others that calm you down when you're stressed. As with external triggers, you need to figure out what circumstances, people, and situations provoke these problematic feelings so that you can avoid them.

Here are some strategies to help you cope positively with your emotions:

- Take deep breaths to calm yourself.

- Write in your journal.

- Play or listen to music; use soothing, soft, or sad music to elicit tears or upbeat music to dance out anger.

- Relax and watch movies; children's videos are soothing.

- Call a support person; family and friends are okay as long as they are not triggers.

- Read inspirational literature or daily meditation books.

- Participate in hobbies or other activities that bring you pleasure.

- Play with your children or pets.

- Paint, sculpt, or do other artwork.

- Listen to or watch relaxation or visualization DVDs and CDs.

- Pray and meditate.

- Attend a Twelve Step meeting or an online Twelve Step chat room.

- Take a shower or bath.

- Walk outside.

- Exercise in any form.

- Look at photographs.

- Read magazines.

- Clean the house.

- Go to a park or natural setting.

- Get a massage or massage yourself.

- Hug yourself.

- Hold a stuffed animal.

Handling anger requires some special techniques. While some of the coping techniques can help, do something physical in order to move the anger through your body. Here are some ideas:

- Yell in the car or into a pillow.
- Hit a soft surface like a big pillow or the bed.
- Rip paper.
- Tear up newspapers or old phone books.
- Mobilize anger into your favorite social causes; for example, Mothers Against Drunk Driving is a great positive channeler of anger.
- Dance out anger.
- Hammer nails; trim shrubs.

Anger sometimes is relieved by destroying objects. If this is the case for you, find a positive outlet:

- Break up old, unwanted dishes or furniture and put them in the garbage.
- Shred by hand old files you no longer need.
- Go to the recycling center and throw glass bottles.

The ground rules for these anger techniques are don't hurt yourself or another person and don't damage anyone's valuable property.

Take some time to list other useful coping strategies. These strategies should include ways to *connect* to your feelings, to your loved ones, and to the world around you. They should include *avenues of self-expression*. They should include *relaxation techniques* to calm and soothe yourself. And they should include ways to *distract yourself* when difficult feelings are triggered that you can't seem to "unplug."

In your notebook or in the space provided in the journal, list other approaches that have helped you in the past or that you would like to experiment with.

DISTORTED THINKING

People with money problems or money addiction tend to have *distorted thinking patterns*. These are patterns of thought that feel real to the person thinking them but are not grounded in reality. A simple example was provided in chapter 7. Remember Tracy, who thought that the best way to get her son off to college was to buy a bigger car to move his stuff with, even though the purchase sank her deeper into debt? That's distorted thinking.

Your recovery depends on your admitting that your thinking is distorted and not realistic. Then you need to alter your unrealistic thinking patterns so that you can recognize that further spending or depriving will not solve your problems.

 YOUR RECOVERY DEPENDS ON YOUR ADMITTING THAT YOUR THINKING IS DISTORTED AND NOT REALISTIC. THEN YOU NEED TO ALTER YOUR UNREALISTIC THINKING PATTERNS SO THAT YOU CAN RECOGNIZE THAT FURTHER SPENDING OR DEPRIVING WILL NOT SOLVE YOUR PROBLEMS.

There's a tendency among people who have money problems to have a limited perspective and to rigidly adhere to false beliefs as the final truth, etched in stone. If this is true for you, you need to identify these distortions as irrational and then challenge them. The way to challenge them is to refute them rationally. In my experience as a therapist, I've found that many clients have similar distorted thinking patterns. The following chart highlights common distortions and offers suggestions for positive and rational ways to think about your situation. When you find yourself thinking these distorted thoughts, replace them with the thoughts suggested here, until you are able to find some that better fit you.

Not all the patterns will apply to you; some are more typical of indulgers, and some are typical of deprivers. Circle the patterns that apply to you, and then work on replacing them with the realistic thought in the right-hand column.

CHART 9-1

Correcting Distorted Thoughts about Money

DEBT	
DISTORTION	**REALITY**
I can't make it without credit cards.	Remember, credit cards are what got me into trouble in the first place.
It is okay to have debt. Everyone has it.	My debt has cost me a lot of money in interest. I cannot handle it. My debts have spiraled out of control.
I will never be in debt.	Debt is a tool for those who can handle it.
Credit cards help me feel that I belong.	I belong to my family and loved ones, not to a bank.
I need a credit card for emergencies.	My debt makes my emergencies even more stressful. I need to save for emergencies.
I am special if I have credit cards. I am in the Platinum Club.	They give cards to everyone now.
I am in debt so I am bad. I am in debt and the whole world is caving in on me. There's no purpose to living because I am in debt. I've made a mess so now I should shrivel up and die.	I am not my debt. Just for today, I am okay. I have my health, my family, my house, my dog, my car, my education. I am okay right now and I will be okay in the future. The world isn't falling in. I will be okay. I can get help, learn new skills, and change my life.

VALUES	
DISTORTION	**REALITY**
I don't need much; I can make do.	It is okay to spend on myself and to enjoy nice things.
People who want money are greedy.	Everyone needs money to live.
I don't bother myself with something as superficial as money.	Money is a part of life that I'm learning to value. Money enables me to achieve dreams.

continued on next page

CHART 9-1

Correcting Distorted Thoughts about Money (continued)

VALUES	
DISTORTION	**REALITY**
Only money matters.	There are many interesting dimensions of life for me to participate in.
I am good because I have expensive tastes.	My expensive tastes have gotten me into trouble.
People will think less of me if I don't have the latest. I want what everyone else has.	I can learn to love my own possessions.

MATERIALISM	
DISTORTION	**REALITY**
If I don't buy it now, there will never be another one as nice.	Nice things are always available, today, tomorrow, and every day after that. Every day offers new opportunities to get nice things. Can I wait?
I have good taste.	I have good taste, but what has it really given me? How can I keep out of debt with my tastes?
I need to spend a lot of money because I know how to enjoy the finer things in life.	These finer things have put a lot of pressure on my partner. They have threatened my relationship.
I know what the superior, expensive things are.	I am not better than others because I have expensive possessions. I will be okay if I buy according to my budget, not my aesthetic talents.
I like to own *the best*.	I have many nice things already. Since I spent so much money on them, I can begin to more fully enjoy my current belongings.
I like nice things.	When I save up in order to buy nicer things, my life is enhanced.

continued on next page

CHART 9-1

Correcting Distorted Thoughts about Money (continued)

SELFHOOD AND IMAGE	
DISTORTION	**REALITY**
I am nothing without money. I am more if I have more money.	I am a worthy person regardless of my money. I know who I am even if I lost my money.
I am worthless because of my debt.	I am not my debt.
I am an exciting person because I keep up with the latest trends.	I am a good person inside. I can be loved for who I am inside.
The people who give me things are the ones who like me the best.	My loved ones have many ways that they express their love and caring for me.
My house, my clothes, my car tell the world that I'm important.	I can express who I am through nonmaterial avenues. I am important because I am alive.

LOVE	
DISTORTION	**REALITY**
If someone really loves me, he or she will pay for me.	Love and money are not the same thing. People express love to me in many ways.
Other people in my life are too concerned with money, not whether I love them.	Other people in my life are concerned about financial pressure because my money habits cause them stress.
I need someone to take care of me financially.	I will still be loved if I am successful with money. It's okay for me to grow up and have power.
Someone always comes through to rescue me.	It is my job to take care of myself, not to expect someone else to rescue me.

continued on next page

CHART 9-1

Correcting Distorted Thoughts about Money (continued)

ENTITLEMENT	
DISTORTION	**REALITY**
I deserve the best.	I deserve the best life possible within my income. My life gets better when I recognize that my troubled relationship with money is partly because I like to believe I'm better than others. I feel insecure about myself, but I can learn to feel secure without having "the best."
I don't deserve anything.	I can be successful with money and have things, too.
I am not good with money.	I can learn to be successful with money. It is okay for me to make good money. I deserve to have a job that I love. I deserve to have a job that pays me enough to live on.
I am not grown up enough to have money.	I can grow up and have money, too.
I hurt my parents when I need money from them. I don't want to put pressure on them.	I am financially dependent on my parents until I reach adulthood. It is realistic for me to expect them to help. They are adults who should take care of me until I become an adult.
My parents owe me.	It is my responsibility to take care of myself when I am old enough to do so.

SECURITY	
DISTORTION	**REALITY**
I have to have money to be okay.	I am okay if I have stuff or if I don't have stuff.
I will never be okay.	I can learn to balance my life and learn about emotional security.
Everyone wants to get my money.	I can determine to whom and what I want to give. I let go when I want to.

continued on next page

CHART 9-1

Correcting Distorted Thoughts about Money (continued)

SECURITY	
DISTORTION	REALITY
People love me more because I buy them nice things.	My true friends love me for me, not for what I can provide them.

ENOUGHNESS	
DISTORTION	REALITY
I never have enough stuff.	There is no real way to say what is "enough." I can learn to distinguish between satisfying what I *need* and what I *want*.
If one is good, two is better.	Having more doesn't mean I am more, especially if I can't afford it.
I need a lot. I am more if I have more.	I am not my money. My money doesn't define who I am. I am fulfilled as I am. I am aware of the fullness of my gifts.
I do not have enough money to pay bills.	I can spend my money and still have some left over in the bank.
There is only so much in the world.	The world is abundant. I am not the best judge of determining what's enough.
I don't have enough to give to others. Everyone wants too much from me.	I have enough to be generous.
I can do what I want because my resources are unlimited.	If I don't use credit tools, I see that my resources truly are limited and I learn to work within them.
I want everything.	I can learn to discern the point of enoughness for me. I can learn to be satisfied and appreciate what I have already.

continued on next page

CHART 9-1

Correcting Distorted Thoughts about Money (continued)

MONEY MANAGEMENT	
DISTORTION	REALITY
Finances are too confusing for me to understand.	I can learn about money. I can ask for help with my finances.
Finances are for grown-up people.	Real grown-ups tackle problems and learn things they don't know.
I can't be bothered with money management.	I can master my finances and not have to be homeless.
I need someone else to control money, because I can't.	I keep control over my own spending; no one else does that for me. I am capable of handling adult responsibilities, so I can handle money also.
I don't want to worry about finances.	I have hurt myself by not attending to my financial needs.
Only losers worry about money.	I need to spend a certain amount of time handling my finances. Money does not consume me.
Money is for spending. I have to spend my money.	I can practice holding on to my money for my real needs.
Money is for saving. I have to save my money.	I need to let go of money in order to live a nice life for myself. I will be okay if I loosen my grip.

POWER AND CONTROL	
DISTORTION	REALITY
My partner can't control money.	I don't have control over another's spending.
My partner doesn't earn enough.	I don't have control over another person's earnings.
If I don't control the money, no one else will.	I can let go of control.
Money is power.	Money is an exchange tool, a vehicle that enables me to survive. I can find appropriate ways to exercise my potency in life.

continued on next page

CHART 9-1

Correcting Distorted Thoughts about Money (continued)

POWER AND CONTROL	
DISTORTION	REALITY
I am powerful when I buy expensive items for myself. The salespeople are impressed with me.	If I spend beyond my means, I make myself less powerful.

Remember, both internal and external circumstances trigger impulsive behavior. People are impulsive because they want to escape difficult circumstances or triggers. The point of identifying triggers is to learn to deal with them in ways other than indulging or depriving.

Let's look now at some techniques to prevent impulsive spending, since this is a common behavioral expression of money problems and money addiction.

Preventing Impulsive Spending

When distorted thoughts are fueled by negative feelings, it's a recipe for out-of-control impulsive urges. Compulsive and impulsive behaviors are factors for every person who has a money problem, whether full-blown money addiction or not. Take a few minutes to reflect on something that you bought on impulse and later regretted. What did you buy that turned out to be a waste of money? Be honest with yourself: those vibrating slippers from a catalog, a computer program you never learned to use, that outfit that never fit. List a few of your financial mistakes. Now as you reflect about those items, what do you feel inside? Let yourself experience these feelings.

Now take a minute to think about a purchase whose pleasure lasted many years. Even if the item is long gone, the memory still makes you happy. What purchases have you made that were good uses of money? List a few of these items: the trip to Disneyland when your kids were young, the piano, the dog, your gardening supplies. What is it like to recall these items? What do you feel? Take some time to savor these sensations, because this is how you should feel about everything you buy. If you don't feel this way about your purchases, you're probably spending impulsively and without conscious awareness.

Impulsive buying is often instigated by the desire to escape powerful emotions. Our pop culture makes light of that connection with slogans like "retail therapy" or the bumper sticker slogan "When the going gets tough, the tough go shopping." For a person with a money disorder, impulsive spending is no joking matter. It has serious consequences for everyone involved, sometimes ripping families apart.

In order to curb impulsivity, first notice how you tend to be triggered. Take a moment to pause and think about what triggered you. Then figure out how to respond to that trigger differently. For example, if you are in the midst of an impulsive purchase (for example, something *not* on your spending plan), then either stall with an interruption at the point of purchase or make sure that next time you have tied your money up so it is inaccessible. Think about ways to keep your money out of reach, such as asking someone you trust to be in charge of your money. Make a list of distractions to prevent you from going to trouble spots in the first place. List methods to get out of trouble spots once you're in them. Keep a handy list of self-soothing techniques to implement when you feel impulsive urges. Relaxation techniques, affirmations, or Twelve Step slogans such as "This too shall pass" are helpful. Some people rely on prayer to help them through difficult times.

Here are some additional suggestions to help you eliminate impulsive spending. You will recognize some of them from the previous chapter's tips for healthy spending and banking guidelines, because they overlap.

- Enlist a trusted friend as a required cosigner on checks.
- Have your paycheck directly deposited to your account.
- Pay with cash only. It's harder to spend cash.
- Put a rubber band around your cash or checkbook, or put them in sealed envelopes to make it more difficult to get at the money.
- Leave extra cash and credit cards at home when shopping.
- Throw catalogs away. Get off mailing lists. Don't sign up for contests. Don't shop online or through shopping networks.
- Have solicitors send information in the mail. Never say yes on the phone without time to think about it.

- Avoid big stores and malls.
- Go to the store fifteen to thirty minutes before closing to prevent distractions and extended shopping time.
- Wait at least twenty-four hours before making a purchase.
- List items needed now. List wanted items. Share these with a friend, family member, or coach. Call that person before buying something from the wanted list.
- Walk around the store with the item in the cart; after a time you may realize you don't need it.
- Don't get chatty with salespeople; it encourages spending.

Your impulsivity costs you money: you end up with junk that you don't need or want. You bought too many gifts, drank too many lattes, and have nothing to show for it. When you impulsively dribble money here and there, your big dreams stay out of reach. If you can't resist every deal that comes along, you'll never accumulate money for greater desires, like travel or expensive hobbies.

It's your own hard-earned cash that you are throwing around. Remember the difficult parts of earning a living: every day you go to a job that you don't always like. The alarm clock, rush hour, your boss, your co-workers, the cutbacks and layoffs—remember all this when you are throwing your money around. You put up with stress for money. Your job may be gloomy or glamorous, but you probably wouldn't show up if someone didn't pay you. *Don't forget that.*

You might be impulsive because you believe that if you don't make the purchase now, the special deal won't be there again, or the item won't be there tomorrow. You feel that this is a once-in-a-lifetime chance and you are special to have this opportunity. Spending money this way can't give you lasting pleasure. Well-thought-out purchases are gratifying and add to one's self-esteem. This pleasure should last the entire life of the product. As you learn to plan your purchases, impulsive shopping becomes less desirable.

You may be impulsive because you have never learned healthy shopping skills. Here's what normal shopping is like: assess what you need, then plan the purchase, then shop for the purchase to compare prices, and then buy the item. For day-to-day items and weekly items such as groceries and household supplies, keep an ongoing shopping list to guide your purchases when you go to these stores. For larger purchases, such as a new coffeemaker, shoes, or a new lamp, refer to your spending plan. Cars, washing machines, and other major purchases require time to research products and compare prices. These skills are not natural for people with a problematic relationship to money.

To monitor your purchases and to figure out whether you are spending impulsively or planfully, you can keep a spending diary. In it, answer the following questions to help you reflect on your purchases. (These questions are also listed in the reproducible journal.)

SPENDING DIARY

1. What did you buy?

2. How did you pay for it?

3. Was it on the spending plan?

4. How did you feel before, during, and after the purchase?

5. What criteria did you use to justify the purchase?
   Do you *need* it or *want* it?

6. Did you tell someone about it beforehand?

7. Whom will this purchase affect? Will that person benefit from it? Suffer because of it?

8. How will this purchase affect your future?

Discussing Purchases before Buying

Some purchases are truly impulsive. Other times purchases begin as a secret yearning inside you. This yearning starts as an imperceptible whisper that gradually builds to a breaking point when you act on the craving. That's how it is with addiction; it's so slick that you yourself don't realize what you are doing. Suddenly it just happens that you are buying something you didn't intend to. Especially in early recovery, your own instincts aren't trustworthy. To help combat this, you need to solicit outside guidance and a second opinion about purchases that are not on your spending plan.

You can implement this a few different ways. The first method is to disclose any purchase over a set amount, say $100, to a trusted confidant (partner, friend, therapist, or sponsor). This keeps you out of secrecy and denial about spending. The second method is to discuss *all* unplanned purchases with your trusted financial helpmate or confidant. For instance, if you decide to buy a new dress for an upcoming wedding, discuss the purchase beforehand, even if you have the money to pay for it. Your financial buddy will help you to brainstorm other options, maybe even look through your existing dresses. You might even set up regular meetings with your trusted confidant to discuss upcoming nonessential purchases.

This honesty isn't natural. First, money is a socially taboo subject. Second, you've probably spent much of your life concealing and lying about how you relate to money. At first, you'll resist this disclosure. That's okay, keep at it. Remember that if you want different results, you have to start acting differently. If discussing purchases before you make them makes you feel vulnerable and strange at first, remind yourself that you are doing it to prevent financial commitments that you later regret.

 REMEMBER, IF YOU FIND YOURSELF HIDING ANYTHING WITH YOUR FINANCES, YOU ARE ON THE SLIPPERY SLOPE OF RELAPSE.

Every week you'll probably discover a new secret intention inside yourself that you don't want to reveal to anyone. If you've been indulging for much of your life and have learned to hide that from other people, you've developed patterns of scheming and concealing that are tied to your urges to spend. When you talk to someone else about your intentions, you break the pattern, and that helps break the urge—and prevent the purchase.

Remember, if you find yourself hiding anything with your finances, you are on the slippery slope of relapse. In recovery, if you keep to your spending plan and can pay for your purchases without affecting anyone else adversely, there is nothing to conceal. You are lying to an invisible enemy. Your recovery depends on your ability to discuss purchases ahead of time.

Identifying and Coping with Relapse

As you identify your triggers and change your thinking, feeling, and behaviors, you will achieve success in overcoming your money addiction. If you're an indulger, you'll get your impulsive spending under control. If you're a depriver, you'll soon feel more comfortable spending up to your plan.

But just as the alcoholic falls off the wagon, you will occasionally have relapses, and you have to learn how to handle them. Roadblocks may impede your progress, and you may find yourself reverting to old behaviors. Life circumstances or unusual triggers come out of nowhere, and you find yourself unable to stay on your spending plan.

Be prepared by knowing the following signs of relapse.

Signs of Relapse

PROCRASTINATION

People with money problems, especially money addicts, tend to be perfectionist black/white or good/bad thinkers. Eventually this perfectionism leads to procrastination. Any slip or mistake causes you to adopt the attitude, "If I can't do it right, I won't do it at all!" You need to repeatedly remind yourself that recovery occurs one day at a time. Debts cannot all be paid back in one day. No one is perfectly recovered, ever! Recovering individuals simply do what's possible today. If you find yourself procrastinating out of fear that you can't do things right, note that you probably will soon be slipping back into trouble.

REVERTING TO DENIAL

You may notice yourself trying hard for a time. Then something mysterious happens and you start to insist that everything's fine, you can handle it, you don't need any more help. Denial is a sure sign of relapse in progress. Remind yourself how bad it felt when you first began the process, and how easy it could be to return to that situation.

RATIONALES

You may begin to express more and more elaborate reasons for choosing to ignore or reinvent your spending plan. Again, you either are or soon will be slipping. Find others who strive to achieve life goals and more profound values, and use their support to help you refocus.

CREATING DRAMAS OR DISTRACTIONS

Personal or familial uproar is a great way to deflect attention away from money problems and money addiction. These dramas distract you from taking ownership of the dysfunction stirring below. If you find yourself "stirring the pot," look for the real cause; you are probably covering up a slip.

JUST STOPPING

Some people quietly tuck their spending plan away. Maybe it feels too hopeless, or you're too ashamed that you can't control your impulses. You just wind up back in trouble. Unfortunately, no one will help you unless you reach out. Your circumstances are ultimately your responsibility. Seek support and don't be ashamed to talk about slipping.

Four Steps to Combat Relapse

There's a four-step process to address your relapse. It involves forgiveness, "feeling" your feelings, controlling the damage, and reinforcing your support system.

STEP 1: FORGIVENESS

The first step is recognition that it's normal to slip and relapse. It's common for addicts to revert to old behaviors. Slips and relapses are a part of the learning process for any recovery. Ask yourself: What have I learned from this? What was it really about? What motivated this behavior? What triggered me to sabotage myself?

Identifying these triggers will help to prevent future relapses. Just get back on the horse and start afresh right now. Mistakes are part of the process. Mistakes help us learn. Forgive yourself and move on.

STEP 2: FEELING THE FEELINGS

With each relapse, you'll become more aware of the pain of the old behavior. Relapses hurt more after you've been clean for a while. On this new path of recovery, you need to experience and articulate your feelings. When you relapse, ask yourself how you feel about the relapse. Are you disappointed in yourself? Is it painful to see how powerless you really are over your own behavior? What negative consequences happen if you continue like this? You'll probably feel a full range of feelings: disappointment, regret, guilt, fear, anger. You now can see how you really can't control this behavior despite all those promises to yourself. It's healthy to feel shame when your behavior is self-destructive or hurtful to others. Let yourself feel this discomfort; it will help you in the future when you're tempted again. With enough of these relapse cycles, you'll be better equipped to anticipate the discomfort and avert it.

You'll also need to bring your awareness inside yourself. Begin to anchor these feelings in your body. Recovery is not an intellectual exercise. Learning to experience your feelings in your body is necessary because it counteracts the numbing, tranquilizing, medicating effect you created through indulging or depriving. Ask yourself what happens in your body when you think about how much money you spent on the couch that wasn't in your spending plan.

STEP 3: CONTROLLING THE DAMAGE

You want to act quickly to alleviate the financial damage of the relapse.

- Is it possible to return the item?
- Is it possible to get out of the financial obligation, or renegotiate it?
- Where will the money come from?
- How will you proceed from here?

It is important to feel the pinch caused by your relapse and to use your support system to help you brainstorm solutions. To contain the negative repercussions, ask your retailer what options you have. Ask friends, family, your therapist, or other support people how they would eliminate financial fallout. It's important to seek outside help; another set of eyes on your situation offers different options.

STEP 4: REINFORCING YOUR SUPPORT SYSTEM

After a relapse, you need to get reengaged with your support system. Tell them about your relapse, and ask for added support. You need people to remind you of the positive consequences of staying on your spending plan and the negative consequences of not repeating old patterns. You need financial helpers to reassure you after relapse.

Over time, you can look forward to the day when your relapses are rare.

How Major Life Events Trigger Relapse

Even when relapses become rare, major life events that affect your financial circumstances can throw you for a loop. Even positive life changes, such as weddings, getting a raise or inheritance, having a child, or retiring, are demanding and stressful and can trigger a descent back to addictive behaviors. These are especially troubling because you don't see them coming. People with money problems and money addicts tend to give themselves permission to act out with celebratory events. Unfortunately, the celebration can be a slippery slope back to the troubled past.

Emergencies that create crisis may also trigger a relapse. The examples here are many and varied: job layoff, health problem, end of a relationship, loss of a parent, natural catastrophe, fight with a boss, family problems, or a midlife identity crisis. Sometimes all you need is one temptation to set you off. You find yourself unable to refuse the offer to open a charge card, tempted by the frequent flyer miles or one-day shopping discount. Or, if you've been a hoarder, you tighten up and quit spending up to plan. You skip dental appointments, tell your child she can't have gymnastic lessons, and so forth.

RELAPSE TRIGGERS ALSO HAPPEN WHEN ONE OF YOUR FRIENDS GETS A RAISE OR AN INHERITANCE. THIS MIGHT TRIGGER LOW SELF-ESTEEM OR ENVY OF YOUR FRIEND'S OPPORTUNITY, WHICH MAY IN TURN TRIGGER OVERSPENDING.

Any type of life stressor or everyday occurrence can trigger a relapse back to dysfunctional behaviors. For example, if the furnace goes out unexpectedly and you only have 25 percent of the funds for it, the stress can set you into relapse. The same goes with a sudden car repair; even if you have the money put aside for it, the scrambling to get to work is stressful. These challenges sometimes trigger denial and possibly credit card use. As a result of the stress, you might "reward" yourself by going on a spending spree. Or you stretch into new territory and plan a vacation. Even if you pay for it in advance, if you don't feel worthy of the pleasure, you might sabotage it by overspending on souvenirs or charging up the credit card when you return home.

Relapse triggers also happen when one of your friends gets a raise or an inheritance. This might trigger low self-esteem or envy of your friend's opportunity, which may in turn trigger overspending. Lastly, a very common relapse trigger is when you've paid off your debts. Now you are at zero, and you might feel that you don't need to adhere to your spending plan any longer. When this happens, it's natural to feel relaxed and a little freer with money, but it's a relapse if you believe that you now can handle and control your money without a plan.

In all these examples, the trance of indulgence or deprivation takes over, and you don't understand what happened.

As you get more practice in handling relapse, you'll get better at pulling out quickly and controlling the damage. You can look forward to the day that relapses are rare. Don't let any one relapse get you down. Your success with it will give you strength to handle or stave off the next.

Summary

Making any type of big change requires dedicated, consistent practice over and over again until new behaviors become habits. Change also involves trial-and-error experimentation until you discover the unique solutions that work for you. Patience with yourself for relapsing is also needed. The more times you come back from relapse and practice the tools, the less often relapses happen, until your money behaviors no longer demand so much attention.

Phase 6, covered in the next chapter, is exciting. Slowly a new sense of the world will emerge in you. That sense is abundance, and it will be worth the work.

• • •

Phase 6: Living the Abundant Life

We now come to the final phase of recovery, living the abundant life. The hard work of recovery always delivers success. Your efforts now demonstrate significant improvement in your finances. If you have been an indulger, your debts are being paid and you have savings accounts. You can carry money in your wallet without spending it. If you've been a depriver, your financial fears no longer motivate your life decisions. You're able to spend on yourself more freely and share your resources with others. If you are a financial underachiever, you are steadily increasing your income. If you are a financial dependent, you've learned to be more responsible about money. The financial improvements for both indulgers and deprivers are visible on the outside for everyone to see.

But recovery doesn't stop at improved freedom with finances; it also grants spiritual, emotional, and mental improvements. In this chapter, we'll take a look at abundance and the limitless gifts of financial recovery, starting with the signs that you have developed a healthy relationship with financial and material matters.

Signs of Financial Health

If you know people who are in remission from cancer, you know that they live with a continuous concern that the cancer may still be there. It can be this way for a person who is in recovery from money problems or a true money addiction; it is hard to know when you are really financially healthy. But just as there are warning signs of relapse, there are telltale signs of health. Here's how you know you are on your way to a healthy relationship with money:

- You no longer keep money secrets.
- You use your spending plan to guide your spending.
- You allow others to help you make adjustments to your spending plan.
- You can pay your bills without credit cards.
- You easily track your earning, spending, and saving.
- You allow others to help you with financial concerns that you don't understand.
- You are able to have frank money discussions with loved ones.
- You feel you are being paid well for your livelihood.
- You use your money to help make your dreams come true.
- Your self-esteem doesn't come from your bank account.
- You are content and enjoy your possessions.
- You can also appreciate new items that come into your life.
- You understand where your trouble spots are and attempt to counteract them.
- You don't fight or argue about money with your spouse or partner.
- You can give generously to others—or not give, if you don't feel the need or don't have the money.
- You can adjust to normal upswings and downswings in finances.
- You have clarity about your own values, not those of your parents, partner, or the culture.
- You are free of the money scripts from your childhood.
- You are on track to maximize your career potential.
- You have hobbies that bring you pleasure.
- You have the ability to maintain healthy money behaviors even in times of stress.

These signs may not mean much to you if you're reading this book and following these steps for the first time. Come back every few months and see how you're doing. You may surprise yourself.

The Sense of Abundance

One of the wonderful things about financial recovery is that as you receive the benefits of material abundance, you experience an abundant state of mind. In other words, cleaning up your finances also gives you the added benefits of psychological, emotional, and spiritual recovery. You learn to trust that there is enough for you to have a good life. You also learn that you yourself are enough. For people recovering from money problems, *abundance* is having the ability to live your life in balance, with flexibility and trust, and in accordance with your authentic values. Abundance is connection to yourself, to your loved ones, to the world around you, because there is no purpose to earning, spending, or saving money if you can't connect to all there is in life. Abundance is discovering your own true worth and purpose. There is no purpose to your life if you can't find some aspect of life that you love more than your bank account, your trimmed lawn, or your car.

Both indulgers and deprivers have unique ways of experiencing abundance, and they have their own growth challenges in recovery. Abundance is the opposite of deprivation and scarcity. So recovery for a depriver requires opening up the channels of material abundance. This is frightening for deprivers, who feel safest while clutching onto the status quo. Deprivers learn to loosen the grip and allow possibilities to expand.

Indulgers, meanwhile, learn to expand the definition of abundance to include nonmaterial outlets. Once unable to experience satisfaction and worth when away from owning or buying things, indulgers find abundance in seeing themselves as whole without these things.

The world is an abundantly gracious place. It is infinitely friendly, grand, and interesting. Our planet is life-giving, vast, and diverse. Scientists tell us that it provides enough food to feed us all, enough trees and mud to house us all. Nature teaches us about death and rebirth. We are a part of this life-giving process, always teeming with possibility, both creation and destruction.

Finding Balance

When you are healthy with your finances, you experience money as a means to a rich, productive life. Money itself isn't the richness; rather, finding balance between money and other intangible aspects of life is.

In chapter 4, we discussed the two spectrums of the money problems

matrix: indulgers/deprivers with relation to material things, and avoiders/
obsessors with relation to wealth and financial matters. Chart 10-1, below, will
remind you of the matrix.

CHART 10-1

The Money Problems Matrix

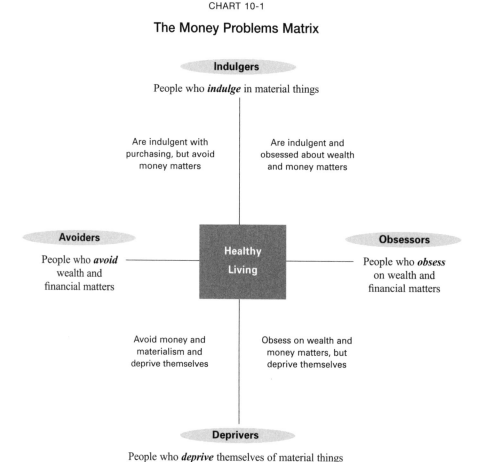

Indulgers

People who *indulge* in material things

Are indulgent with
purchasing, but avoid
money matters

Are indulgent and
obsessed about wealth
and money matters

Avoiders

People who *avoid*
wealth and
financial matters

**Healthy
Living**

Obsessors

People who *obsess*
on wealth and
financial matters

Avoid money and
materialism and
deprive themselves

Obsess on wealth and
money matters, but
deprive themselves

Deprivers

People who *deprive* themselves of material things

Healthy living is at the center point of the grid. The farther you move from
the center, the deeper and more desperate your problems with material goods
and financial matters are apt to be. The goal of recovery, contentment, and
abundance is found at the center point of this matrix. The balance point is
somewhere between the four points. You don't want to lavish yourself with
unnecessary things, nor should you deprive yourself of experiencing the richness

of the world. You don't want to obsess on wealth and financial matters, nor do you want to avoid them. The proverb "A rich man is a man who knows he has enough" says it perfectly: the center of the grid is the point of enoughness.

When you live in the center, you responsibly take care of material needs without going overboard. You know you are not insatiable because you have found a balance point for yourself between striving and restraining. This is an inner state of satisfaction and contentment; it isn't necessarily about having more money. It can be achieved at any income level.

You also find a balance between avoiding and fixating on money management. You now spend adequate time on your finances so that money doesn't cause problems for you or your relationships. Avoiders are no longer afraid to take responsibility for handling money. Obsessors can let go of material obsessions and experience other types of riches in life. Each person recognizes money as a necessary part of life that needs appropriate attention. This balance point frees you up to experience the full range of life's riches. When you have this balance point, your money concerns don't cause trouble in your relationships.

Flexibility and Trust

In recovery, you learn to be flexible and to trust. This is especially important for people who have struggled with money problems, because financial circumstances constantly change. Sometimes things happen in life that cost extra money; sometimes opportunities come our way. Life is constantly filled with ups and downs. Abundance is being able to flex and flow with these changes without a disruption to your inner peace. The winds can shift direction at any time, so it's best not to become too attached to financial gains or losses. The goal is not rigid perfection; it is to become adaptable to changes.

You may take many forward steps and then backslide. This is natural, so you get back up and try again. When you live an abundant life, you understand that you have only some control over things in your life; you cannot fully control money, so you shouldn't hold on too tightly. Trust is the key. The economy goes up: your serenity and trust remains the same. The stock market and your investments take a dip: you stay steady. Applications for higher-paying jobs yield no returns: you keep trying.

Abundance, like life, gets off course at times, and you are able to accept this as a normal part of a growth process. Regardless of the bumps and distractions, you feel secure and confident of the forward movement.

Emotional Authenticity

You cannot live richly and well unless you know who you are and what makes you happy. There's really no benefit to having material wealth if you do not know how to use it. In early recovery, you began to clarify some of your goals and values. Now it's time to discover your own feelings and beliefs—the ones that make you unique. What excites you? What saddens you? What frustrates you? What brings you hope? What emotions do you feel most often? What do you love more than anything in the world? What special qualities make you the person you are?

You may not be a famous movie star or a trendsetter, yet there is a rich purpose living inside you. There are things inside you that only you feel. There are things in the world that only you can see. What parts of life do you see and feel that no one else can see or feel?

 IF YOU WANT RECOVERY FROM MONEY PROBLEMS, YOU MUST DISCOVER WHO YOU ARE, AND YOU MUST REMAIN COMMITTED TO THAT JOURNEY, WHEREVER IT TAKES YOU.

Abundance is having an unflinching dedication to your own unique essence. If you want recovery from money problems, you must discover who you are, and you must remain committed to that journey, wherever it takes you. Probably it will wind around many twists and turns. Hang on; it has more to offer you than any shopping mall ever could.

So look around and see what makes you purr. Ultimately we only find rest when we experience our own inner essence. Connecting to your heart and your love, your mind and your ideas, your body and its movements will bring you the inner security that you are looking for. Recovery offers you the confidence to be yourself and live your path the way no one else can.

A Unique Lifestyle

Knowing who you are is part of the equation. You also must find unique avenues to express your essence through your lifestyle. As a psychologist, I am surprised when clients feel bored or depressed with life. It shocks me because I believe we live in an amazingly interesting world, with unending possibilities for personal gratification. Sometimes I fantasize standing up and shouting, "Go dress up and act out the Civil War, or learn how to grow bonsai trees, or be a docent at the nature center, or play basketball at the community center." There are old people in nursing homes to visit, vintage cars to refurbish, festivals to attend, theater companies that need sets painted, people you can teach to read and write, and your own genealogy to research. There are classes to take, homeless to feed, species to save, sweaters to knit, and pyramids to visit. *There is no end to life's bountiful offerings.*

Indeed there are outlets for every temperament—introverts and social animals alike. You can choose to be a spectator or a participant: watch drag races or be the driver. You can choose to make your involvement light or deep: take a day hike or trek the Continental Divide. You may be passionately interested in only one or two issues; you may dabble in many activities. Regardless of your involvement, if you want full recovery, you must find and participate in fun, pleasurable activities. These activities should uniquely reflect your personality, interests, and values.

You'll need to find hobbies, creative or artistic expression, social clubs, physical outlets, and intellectual stimulation. Some people find meaning and pleasure by giving back through volunteer work, some by learning new skills. If you don't know what you love, go to the library and look through the hobby section, browse the community education program for classes of interest, scan the community calendar for events, or ask at your house of worship. Go back to review your life vision in chapter 8 and see what interests popped out there.

Your unique blend of interests may or may not involve spending money. If you don't have the money to start, find free venues or brainstorm ways to participate in these activities today without spending a lot of money. Get creative; look for cheaper, downscaled versions and alternative options. Start small if you need to: a group lesson rather than private lessons, a weekend camping trip instead of a $3,000 cruise. In the meantime, put it in your spending plan so you can save toward it.

Just remember, abundance is all around you. Find the things that you love; dive in and create your unique lifestyle.

Relationships

The experts who study terminally ill and dying patients tell us that at the end of life, the dying speak of regrets in relationships, not material achievement or acquisition. In the end, it's the people we love and who love us back that matter, not things. At the end, we say good-bye to people, not things. When there is nothing left to achieve or accomplish in the world, we remember our connections. Everything else fades into the distance.

Think deep and hard about your ability to relate and connect to those you love. Take time to reflect on the following questions. You may want to write the answers in the space provided in the journal.

- Whom do you feel connected to? What is it like for you to be connected to them? Have you expressed your feelings of connection to them? Why or why not?

- Whom have you lost connection with? What is that like? Do you feel okay about losing the connection?

- Who has influenced you? Have you told them? Why or why not? Whom do you try to influence? How do you do this? Why do you want to be an influence for them?

- Who has opened you to love more fully? Have you told them? Why or why not? How could you love them more fully?

- Who loves you? How do you receive love from them? What is that like for you? Do they know what their love means to you?

- Who are the people you love? How do you demonstrate your love? Do you express it enough? Do they know it?

Imagine a society in which wealth was measured by the quality of your relationships. If you think that money is the only avenue of wealth, this definition is helpful. So start to cultivate gratitude for the people in your life. However, there's more to wealth than quantity, even when it comes to quantities of friends. One true friend who knows you and accepts you probably contributes more to your inner worth than many nonintimate acquaintances. Wealth can be measured both through quantity of relationship as well as quality of relationship. So aim for deeper and more authentic relationships—as well as more connections.

Love is gold worth pursuing. Some find love in God, some find love in romantic partners, and some find love with their children or pets. Learn to stretch your ability to give and receive love. Start sharing yourself. Start with yourself, then your family, then the world around you. Emotionally generous people receive a lot back. It's natural to take care of those we love and the world around us. It is aberrant to withhold love and resources.

Finding True Abundance Within

It is beneath our humanity to derive a life and a lifestyle at the shopping mall or by hoarding up piles of goods and money. We are greater than that. Until now, we just didn't know how or where to find our true worth. We were seduced into thinking money and the things it could buy would make us whole. We were vulnerable to any type of hopeful promise of pain reduction. It's as old as time to be tricked with worldly goods: the Hindus call it maya; the Christians say it is easier for a camel to go through the eye of a needle than for a rich man to enter the kingdom of heaven. Where once we just listened to those wise words, we now understand.

The stuff we buy breaks and decays and fills landfills. The money we hoard does no good for anyone. That stuff could never offer enough because it was never what we wanted. Abundance can't be purchased at the mall.

You yourself are the most valuable possession you will ever bear witness to. Your unique thoughts, dreams, visions, gifts, limits, challenges, and feelings are your greatest possessions, and they are yours alone. This was the miracle that came alive on the day you were born. You bring something to the world that no one else can. Regardless of how much money you have, how healthy or dysfunctional you are or have been with money, money could never bring you yourself. Accumulating it, losing it, avoiding it, grabbing for it—money could never deliver contentment and peace. Money was always an illusion; it wasn't you. Antoine de Saint-Exupéry said, "What is essential is invisible to the eye." What is really essential is what is under your money games, your money scripts, your piles of money, or your piles of debt. Under all that is a unique self-longing to be excavated, to be set free. There are talents and gifts to share. The world needs your contribution.

You came to this book because you have a troubled relationship with money and material things. Deal with your money so you can get on with the important business of living your life authentically. Deal with your dysfunctional thoughts and feelings so you can experience all of life's offerings. There is so much to life, and it all costs so little. Your financial recovery will teach you to align your money with your inner values. If you feel the unique purpose for your life, then you'll be able to see money for what it is: a means of exchange, a vehicle. Money isn't nearly as interesting as life is.

Your future is waiting for you to step into it.

And we are waiting to hear the song that only you can sing.

・ ・ ・

Appendixes

Are You Codependent?

The first person to feel the pinch of a money addiction or money problems is often a spouse or family member. It's often the partner who feels the pain of the debt or the hoarding. Sometimes the coping mechanism for the pain is to become codependent. This is always problematic. A codependent derives self-esteem from controlling the emotions and financial behaviors of the addict. Codependents support, unconsciously encourage, or "enable" the problem user's or addict's behavior.

To discern financial codependency, answer the following questions in your notebook or journal.

1. Do you feel responsible for a loved one's behavior? Describe.

2. Do you try to fix or control the loved one's behavior? Describe.

3. Are you unable to say no to your loved ones? Describe.

4. Have you adjusted your spending and/or saving in any way to meet the loved one's demands? Describe.

If you believe you are codependent, you need to begin to look at the severity of your enabling behavior. The following questions address the dynamics of the codependent relationship and highlight the codependent's contribution to the financial dysfunction.

1. Have you covered up for your partner's dysfunctional money behaviors? Why?

2. Have you spent less than you normally would in order to compensate for the overspending of your partner? Give examples.

3. Have you made any adjustments to your income in order to accommodate the money-related behaviors of a loved one? For example, have you taken on additional work or a second job?

4. Have you ever asked a third party for money to pay your partner's debts?

5. Have you risked your own credit rating to help your partner?

6. Have you ever overdrawn your own bank account or put yourself into financial jeopardy to pay your partner's debts?

7. Have you ever argued with your partner about his or her money-related behaviors?

8. Have you ever secretly checked the bills and receipts of your partner to determine his or her spending habits?

9. Have you ever avoided looking at bills, receipts, and the like, even though you have concerns about your partner's financial problems?

10. Have you ever avoided discussions because you don't want to put pressure on your partner?

11. Have you avoided asking how much your parner earns?

12. Has your partner broken promises to you about financial behavior? If so, have you given him or her second, third, or fourth chances?

13. Do you view your partner as incapable of managing his or her own finances?

14. Do you avoid asking your partner specifics about how he or she manages his or her money?

15. Do you view your partner as dependent on you in order to be competent—for example, do you help him or her get a better job or pass tests?

16. Have you ever borrowed from others or depleted your savings to pay off your partner's debts?

17. Have you deprived yourself in order to compensate for your partner's behavior?

Your answers to these questions will help you determine if you are co-dependently involved with a problem user or a money addict. If you answered yes to six or more questions, it's likely that you have attempted to control or fix your loved one's problems. In doing this, you've unwittingly participated in another's destructive money behaviors. If this is the case, it's imperative for you to redirect your helping behavior to yourself.

If you are codependent, you probably derive a lot of satisfaction from helping others. This makes it difficult for you to recognize that you yourself need help, too. Consider attending therapy or support groups such as Co-Dependents Anonymous (CoDA) or Al-Anon. You might also find the books *Codependent No More* by Melody Beattie and *Facing Codependence* by Pia Mellody to be helpful.

. . .

The Signs of Compulsive Debting

Consider these twelve signs of a compulsive debtor. If you relate to them, then Debtors Anonymous might be right for you.

1. Being unclear about your financial situation: not knowing account balances, monthly expenses, loan interest rates, fees, fines, or contractual obligations.

2. Frequently "borrowing" items such as books, pens, or small amounts of money from friends and others, then failing to return them.

3. Poor saving habits: not planning for taxes, retirement, or other not recurring but predictable items, and then feeling surprised when they come due; a "live for today, don't worry about tomorrow" attitude.

4. Compulsive shopping: being unable to pass up a "good deal," making impulsive purchases, leaving price tags on clothes so they can be returned, not using items you've purchased.

5. Difficulty in meeting basic financial or personal obligations, and/or an inordinate sense of accomplishment when such obligations are met.

6. A different feeling when buying things on credit than when paying cash, a feeling of being in the club, of being accepted, of being grown up.

7. Living in chaos and drama around money: using one credit card to pay another, bouncing checks, always having a financial crisis to contend with.

8. A tendency to live on the edge: living paycheck to paycheck, taking risks with health and car insurance coverage, writing checks hoping money will appear to cover them.

9. Unwarranted inhibition and embarrassment in what should be a normal discussion of money.

10. Overworking or underearning: working extra hours to earn money to pay creditors, using time inefficiently, taking jobs below your skill and education level.

11. An unwillingness to care for and value yourself: living in self-imposed deprivation, denying your basic needs in order to pay your creditors.

12. A feeling or hope that someone will take care of you if necessary so you won't really get into serious financial trouble, that there will always be someone you can turn to.

Forms and Blank Worksheets

Debt Worksheet 189

Spending Plan Worksheet 191

Six-Month Worksheet 197

Shaving Worksheet 203

Weekly Income and Expense Tracker 209

These forms are also included in the free reproducible journal. Go to hazelden.org/bookstore. On the *Spent* page, click on "reproducible journal with worksheets" to download the journal.

Debt Worksheet

Debt	Total Amount Due	Finance Charge (Percent)	Minimum Payments	Date of Last Payment	Other Comments
Credit Cards					
Other Debts					
Car Loan #1					
Car Loan #2					
Equity Line #1					
Equity Line #2					
Utilities					

Debt Worksheet (continued)

Debt	Total Amount Due	Finance Charge (Percent)	Minimum Payments	Date of Last Payment	Other Comments
Medical Bills					
Services					
Personal Debts					
TOTAL					

Spending Plan Worksheet

Month _____

Expense	Cash	Checkbook	Credit Card 1	Credit Card 2	Total	Spending Plan Goal	Difference
Shelter							
Rent or Mortgage							
Property Taxes							
Property Insurance							
Heat							
Utilities							
Telephone							
Water							
Décor							
Replacements, Purchases							
Maintenance, Cleaning							
Garden Supplies							
Garbage Collection							
Association Fees							
Other							
Other							
Transportation							
Car Payment 1							
Car Payment 2							
Insurance							
Gasoline							
Maintenance, Cleaning							
License							
Bus, Taxi, Tolls, Parking							
Other							
Other							

Spending Plan Worksheet (continued)

Expense	Cash	Checkbook	Credit Card 1	Credit Card 2	Total	Spending Plan Goal	Difference
Food							
Groceries							
Delivered Goods, e.g., Pizza							
Snacks							
Work Lunches							
School Lunches							
Other							
Other							
Clothing							
Personal							
Spouse or Partner							
Children							
Maintenance, Cleaning							
Other							
Other							
Entertainment							
Vacations							
Meals Out							
Movies, Plays, Music							
Hobbies							
Spectator Sports							
Sports Equipment, Toys							
Electronic Equipment							
TV, Cable TV, Public TV							
Other							
Other							

Spending Plan Worksheet (continued)

Expense	Cash	Checkbook	Credit Card 1	Credit Card 2	Total	Spending Plan Goal	Difference
Savings (DEPOSITS INTO ACCOUNTS)							
Credit Union, Bank							
Education							
Retirement							
Contingency							
Other							
Other							
Health							
Insurance							
Doctor							
Dentist							
Medications							
Therapy, Massage							
Exercise Classes, Equipment							
Other							
Other							
Education							
Lessons, Tuition							
Books, Papers, Magazines							
Supplies							
Other							
Other							

Spending Plan Worksheet (continued)

Expense	Cash	Checkbook	Credit Card 1	Credit Card 2	Total	Spending Plan Goal	Difference
Family							
Life Insurance							
Legal							
Child Care: Daily							
Child Care: Occasional							
Allowances							
Gifts							
Holidays							
Pets: Food and Supplies							
Pets: Vet Care							
Other							
Other							
Donations							
House of Worship							
Political							
Charitable							
Other							
Other							
Personal							
Barber, Beauty Shop							
Toiletries							
Postage							
Alcohol							
Computer: Purchase, Repair							
Computer: Software, Supplies							
Other							
Other							

Spending Plan Worksheet (continued)

Expense	Cash	Checkbook	Credit Card 1	Credit Card 2	Total	Spending Plan Goal	Difference
Installment Payments							
Credit Card 1							
Credit Card 2							
Department Store							
Student Loan							
Other							
Miscellaneous							
Union and Membership Dues							
Taxes: Social Security							
Federal Income							
State Income							
Local Income							
Unreimbursed Business Expenses							
Other							
TOTAL OUTGO							

Income	Amount
Paycheck 1	
Paycheck 2	
Dividends	
Interest	
Social Security	
Pension	
Gifts	
Other	
TOTAL INCOME	

195

Six-Month Worksheet

Enter the totals for six months (if possible) of your expenses and income on this worksheet.
Compute the total, then divide the total by the number of months entered to get the monthly average.

Expense	Month 1	Month 2	Month 3	Month 4	Month 5	Month 6	Total	Number of Months Entered	Monthly Average
Shelter									
Rent or Mortgage									
Property Taxes									
Property Insurance									
Heat									
Utilities									
Telephone									
Water									
Décor									
Replacements, Purchases									
Maintenance, Cleaning									
Garden Supplies									
Garbage Collection									
Association Fees									
Other									
Other									
Transportation									
Car Payment 1									
Car Payment 2									
Insurance									
Gasoline									
Maintenance, Cleaning									
License									
Bus, Taxi, Tolls, Parking									
Other									
Other									

Six-Month Worksheet (continued)

Expense	Month 1	Month 2	Month 3	Month 4	Month 5	Month 6	Total	Number of Months Entered	Monthly Average
Food									
Groceries									
Delivered Goods, e.g., Pizza									
Snacks									
Work Lunches									
School Lunches									
Other									
Other									
Clothing									
Personal									
Spouse or Partner									
Children									
Maintenance, Cleaning									
Other									
Other									
Entertainment									
Vacations									
Meals Out									
Movies, Plays, Music									
Hobbies									
Spectator Sports									
Sports Equipment, Toys									
Electronic Equipment									
TV, Cable TV, Public TV									
Other									
Other									

Six-Month Worksheet (continued)

Expense	Month 1	Month 2	Month 3	Month 4	Month 5	Month 6	Total	Number of Months Entered	Monthly Average
Savings (DEPOSITS INTO ACCOUNTS)									
Credit Union, Bank									
Education									
Retirement									
Contingency									
Other									
Other									
Health									
Insurance									
Doctor									
Dentist									
Medications									
Therapy, Massage									
Exercise Classes, Equipment									
Other									
Other									
Education									
Lessons, Tuition									
Books, Papers, Magazines									
Supplies									
Other									
Other									

Six-Month Worksheet (continued)

Expense	Month 1	Month 2	Month 3	Month 4	Month 5	Month 6	Total	Number of Months Entered	Monthly Average
Family									
Life Insurance									
Legal									
Child Care: Daily									
Child Care: Occasional									
Allowances									
Gifts									
Holidays									
Pets: Food and Supplies									
Pets: Vet Care									
Other									
Other									
Donations									
House of Worship									
Political									
Charitable									
Other									
Other									
Personal									
Barber, Beauty Shop									
Toiletries									
Postage									
Alcohol									
Computer: Purchase, Repair									
Computer: Software, Supplies									
Other									
Other									

Six-Month Worksheet (continued)

Expense	Month 1	Month 2	Month 3	Month 4	Month 5	Month 6	Total	Number of Months Entered	Monthly Average
Installment Payments									
Credit Card 1									
Credit Card 2									
Department Store									
Student Loan									
Other									
Miscellaneous									
Union and Membership Dues									
Taxes: Social Security									
Federal Income									
State Income									
Local Income									
Unreimbursed Business Expenses									
Other									
TOTAL OUTGO									

Income	Month 1	Month 2	Month 3	Month 4	Month 5	Month 6	Total	Number of Months Entered	Monthly Average
Paycheck 1									
Paycheck 2									
Dividends									
Interest									
Social Security									
Pension									
Gifts									
Other									
TOTAL INCOME									

Shaving Worksheet

Use this worksheet to shave your six-month spending averages to fit your goals. To do this, fill in your six-month spending averages in column A. Put your goal in column C. Figure out how much you will have to increase or decrease the amount and insert this in column B.

Expense	A Six-Month Spending Average	B Adjustment (Reduction in Plan)	C New Spending Plan
Shelter			
Rent or Mortgage			
Property Taxes			
Property Insurance			
Heat			
Utilities			
Telephone			
Water			
Décor			
Replacements, Purchases			
Maintenance, Cleaning			
Garden Supplies			
Garbage Collection			
Association Fees			
Other			
Other			
Transportation			
Car Payment 1			
Car Payment 2			
Insurance			
Gasoline			
Maintenance, Cleaning			
License			
Bus, Taxi, Tolls, Parking			
Other			
Other			

Shaving Worksheet (continued)

Expense	A Six-Month Spending Average	B Adjustment (Reduction in Plan)	C New Spending Plan
Food			
Groceries			
Delivered Goods, e.g., Pizza			
Snacks			
Work Lunches			
School Lunches			
Other			
Other			
Clothing			
Personal			
Spouse or Partner			
Children			
Maintenance, Cleaning			
Other			
Other			
Entertainment			
Vacations			
Meals Out			
Movies, Plays, Music			
Hobbies			
Spectator Sports			
Sports Equipment, Toys			
Electronic Equipment			
TV, Cable TV, Public TV			
Other			
Other			
Savings (DEPOSITS INTO ACCOUNTS)			
Credit Union, Bank			
Education			
Retirement			
Contingency			
Other			
Other			

Shaving Worksheet (continued)

Expense	A Six-Month Spending Average	B Adjustment (Reduction in Plan)	C New Spending Plan
Health			
Insurance			
Doctor			
Dentist			
Medications			
Therapy, Massage			
Exercise Classes, Equipment			
Other			
Other			
Education			
Lessons, Tuition			
Books, Papers, Magazines			
Supplies			
Other			
Other			
Family			
Life Insurance			
Legal			
Child Care: Daily			
Child Care: Occasional			
Allowances			
Gifts			
Holidays			
Pets: Food and Supplies			
Pets: Vet Care			
Other			
Other			
Donations			
House of Worship			
Political			
Charitable			
Other			
Other			

Shaving Worksheet (continued)

Expense	A Six-Month Spending Average	B Adjustment (Reduction in Plan)	C New Spending Plan
Personal			
Barber, Beauty Shop			
Toiletries			
Postage			
Alcohol			
Computer: Purchase, Repair			
Computer: Software, Supplies			
Other			
Other			
Installment Payments			
Credit Card 1			
Credit Card 2			
Department Store			
Student Loan			
Other			
Other			
Miscellaneous			
Union and Membership Dues			
Taxes: Social Security			
Federal Income			
State Income			
Local Income			
Unreimbursed Business Expenses			
Other			
Other			
TOTAL OUTGO			

Shaving Worksheet (continued)

	Amount
Income	
Paycheck 1	
Paycheck 2	
Dividends	
Interest	
Social Security	
Pension	
Gifts	
Other	
Other	
TOTAL INCOME	

PAGE 5 OF 5

Notes

_____

_____

_____

_____

_____

_____

_____

_____

Weekly Income and Expense Tracker

The Weekly Income and Expense Tracker is an optional way to plan. It helps you plan your payments for the month. It is divided into four columns, one for each week of the month.

1 Start by entering your checking account balance (cash in bank) and add any deposits to be made during the month. This gives you the total cash available to pay bills with this week.

2 Then fill in every bill to be paid during the month in the weekly column for which it's due. Remember to include grocery money, gas, and any other weekly expenses. Add the bills' amounts to obtain the total amount due.

3 Subtract the total amount of bills to be paid from the total cash available.

4 After you have subtracted the total amount of bills due from the total cash available, you'll have a remaining amount. This remaining amount gets transferred to the next week, under cash in bank. Remember, if you have a big bill due the second, third, or fourth week of the month, you'll need to carry over money from the previous weeks to cover it.

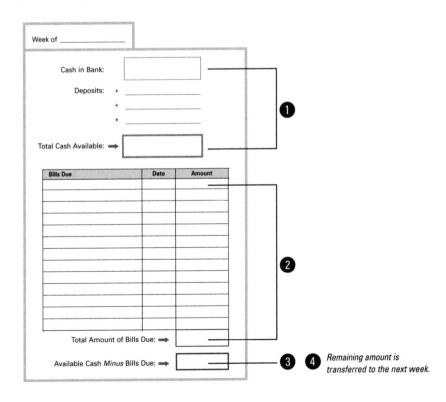

Weekly Income and Expense Tracker

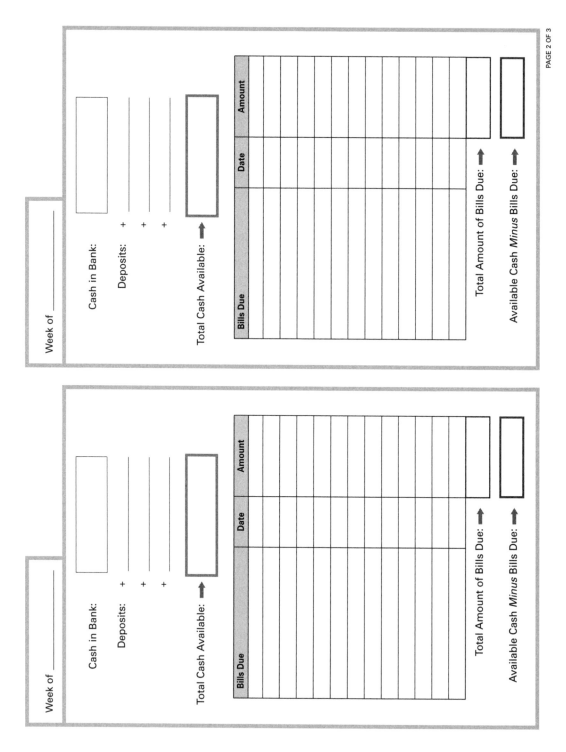

Week of _____

Cash in Bank:

Deposits:
+
+
+

Total Cash Available: ➤

Bills Due	Date	Amount

Total Amount of Bills Due: ➤

Available Cash *Minus* Bills Due: ➤

Week of _____

Cash in Bank:

Deposits:
+
+
+

Total Cash Available: ➤

Bills Due	Date	Amount

Total Amount of Bills Due: ➤

Available Cash *Minus* Bills Due: ➤

Weekly Income and Expense Tracker

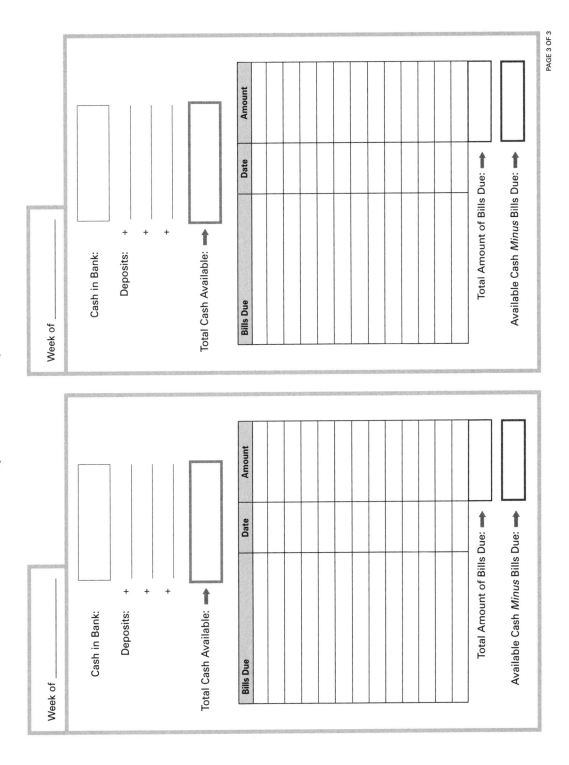

Week of _____

Cash in Bank: _____

Deposits: _____ +

_____ +

_____ +

Total Cash Available: ➡ _____

Bills Due	Date	Amount

Total Amount of Bills Due: ➡ _____

Available Cash *Minus* Bills Due: ➡ _____

Week of _____

Cash in Bank: _____

Deposits: _____ +

_____ +

_____ +

Total Cash Available: ➡ _____

Bills Due	Date	Amount

Total Amount of Bills Due: ➡ _____

Available Cash *Minus* Bills Due: ➡ _____

Resources

Debtors Anonymous, a Twelve Step Program

www.debtorsanonymous.org, 800-421-2383, 781-453-2743

Pros: If you feel your problem has grown beyond your own ability to help yourself, then consider seeking help from Debtors Anonymous. It benefits all types of problem money behaviors through education about addiction, and it provides group support for changing your behaviors pertaining to finances. Additionally, because financial resources are limited for many money addicts, a Twelve Step program is a low-cost alternative to therapy. It's an opportunity to surround yourself with people who are attempting to live differently with money. There is online support if you live in an area without meetings.

Cons: Twelve Step programs may not be readily available for you. They are organized by laypersons, who are untrained to deal with your other psychological problems or your legal situations. Sometimes shame about financial circumstances prevents a person from attending group meetings.

Consumer Credit Counselors

Green Path Credit Counseling, www.greenpath.com, 800-550-1961

Pros: Consumer credit counseling associations have become very accessible. If you elect to use a credit counseling organization, check its track record first. Make sure it is credible. These organizations are beneficial for many because they negotiate with the credit card companies for you. Sometimes they are able to arrange lower interest rates and get your total payoff amount lowered. Credit counseling organizations are sometimes less costly than other professional services.

Cons: Because this is a new industry and isn't regulated tightly, some companies are not reputable. They are trained to work with your financial situation, but have minimal training in recognizing or responding to long-standing behavioral patterns. They focus exclusively on paying off debts rather than teaching you to live in balance.

Financial Planners

Financial Planners Association, www.fpanet.org, 800-322-4237

Pros: Financial planners are very important for your long-term planning. They guide you in making projections about your future needs and goals. They can help you to make financial decisions about your savings, retirement, inheritance, business arrangements, and many other areas.

Cons: Financial planners may not understand your psychological relationship with money. Be sure to find one who is well-versed in psychological and behavioral finance.

Marital Counseling

American Association for Marriage and Family Therapy, www.aamft.org, 703-838-9808
Imago Relationships International, www.gettingtheloveyouwant.com, 800-729-1121

Pros: If you are lying to your spouse or partner about money or if that person is endangering the children, for example by spending food money, clothing budget, or college savings or stealing from children's piggy banks or savings accounts, you should consider bringing your partner to marital counseling. A third party can assist you with communicating your concerns to your partner.

Cons: Marital counseling can be expensive and might not be effective with your financial situation.

Career Counseling

Many local colleges and community colleges offer career counseling.

Pros: Career counseling is useful for those who haven't advanced in their job or are in the wrong career for them. Some people need further schooling to increase income, guidance about finding a satisfying profitable career, or retraining due to a layoff. Career counselors can also help you to create an effective résumé or coach you to negotiate your salary. You can often find it free at college and career placement centers.

Cons: Private career counseling can be expensive.

Further Psychiatric Help

Check your health care provider for a referral.

Pros: You might need psychological testing or a psychiatric evaluation to assess any complications about your financial behavior. These professionals help you to rule out any overlapping psychological diagnosis, such as depression, anxiety, bipolar disorder, and attention deficit/hyperactivity disorder. Some of these debilitating disorders might prevent you from fully succeeding at your financial recovery.

A qualified professional will also help you to rule out addictions. Because addictions are expensive, your financial troubles might be the secondary effect of a primary addiction, such as a gambling, sex, or drug addiction.

Cons: Psychological and psychiatric evaluations are expensive and might not be covered by insurance.

Psychotherapy

American Psychological Association, www.apa.org, 800-374-2721, 202-336-5500
American Psychiatric Association, www.psych.org, 703-907-7300
Attention Deficit Disorders: Children and Adults with Attention Deficit/Hyperactivity Disorder, www.chadd.org, 800-233-4050, 301-306-7070
Attention Deficit Disorder Association, www.add.org, 856-439-9099
Depression and Bipolar Support Alliance, www.dbsalliance.org, 800-826-3632

Pros: Psychotherapy offers you support to explore your problem in depth. Psychotherapists are trained to work with your whole story, not just your finances. If you are properly educated about money, psychotherapy will help you to grow spiritually and gain greater meaning in life while balancing the fiscal part of life.

Cons: A psychotherapist may not understand the financial side of your situation, so you will need other assistance to deal with that.

Twelve Step Resources

Alcoholics Anonymous, www.alcoholics-anonymous.org, 212-870-3400
Narcotics Anonymous World Services, www.na.org, 818-773-9999
Food Addicts Anonymous, www.foodaddictsanonymous.org, 561-967-3871
Overeaters Anonymous, www.oa.org, 505-891-2664
Debtors Anonymous, www.debtorsanonymous.org, 800-421-2383, 781-453-2743
Gamblers Anonymous, www.gamblersanonymous.org, 213-386-8789
Co-Dependents Anonymous, www.codependents.org, 602-277-7991
(answering service only)

Clutterers Anonymous, www.clutterersanonymous.net, 310-281-6064
Workaholics Anonymous, www.workaholics-anonymous.org, 510-273-9253

Accountants/Bookkeepers

American Institute of Certified Public Accountants, www.aicpa.org, 212-596-6200
American Institute of Professional Bookkeepers, www.aipb.org, 800-622-0121

Pros: If you aren't good at math, consider hiring a bookkeeper or an accountant to help you with it. If the cost is prohibitive, consider hiring an accounting student.

Cons: Accountants work only with the financial side of your situation. Combine this help with appropriate therapy or a Twelve Step resource when possible.

• • •

❖ Notes ❖

Chapter 1

1. Michael F. Jacobson and Laurie Ann Mazur, *Marketing Madness: A Survival Guide for a Consumer Society* (Boulder, CO: Westview Press, 1995), 13.

2. Adapted from Juliet Schor, *The Overspent American: Upscaling, Downshifting, and the New Consumer* (New York: Basic Books, 1998).

3. Adapted from Barry Schwartz, *The Paradox of Choice: Why More Is Less* (New York: HarperPerennial, 2004).

Chapter 2

1. José Garcia, James Lardner, and Cindy Zeldin, *Up to Our Eyeballs: How Shady Lenders and Failed Economic Policies Are Drowning Americans in Debt* (New York: New Press, 2008).

2. Ben Woolsey and Matt Schulz, "Credit Card Industry Facts, Debt Statistics 2006–2008," Credit Card News Archive, www.creditcards.com/credit-card-news/credit-card-industry-facts-personal-debt-statistics-1276.php.

3. Peter S. Goodman, "Uncomfortable Answers to Questions on the Economy," *New York Times,* July 19, 2008.

4. Tamara Draut, "Economic State of Young America," Spring 2008, Demos: A Network for Ideas and Action, www. demos.org/pubs/esya_web.pdf.

5. Tamara Draut and Javier Silva, "Generation Broke: The Growth of Debt Among Young Americans," Oct. 2004; Ellen Braune and Timothy Rusch, "Generation Broke: Crushing Debt Burden Takes Toll on Generation X," Oct. 21, 2004, available at http://archive.demos.org/page193.cfm.

6. U.S. Courts, "1987–2003 Fiscal Year Bankruptcy Filings by Chapter and District," Bankruptcy Statistics, www.uscourts.gov/bnkrpctystats/FY1987_2003.pdf; U.S. Courts, "1990–2002 Calendar Year Bankruptcy Filings by Chapter and District," Bankruptcy Statistics, www.uscourts.gov/bnkrpctystats/Bk2002_1990Calendar.pdf.

7. Jeannine Aversa, Associated Press, "Report by the Mortgage Bankers Association," *The Detroit News,* June 6, 2008.

8. Schor, *The Overspent American.*

9. Roger W. Ferguson, Jr., "Questions and Reflections on the Personal Saving Rate," remarks to the National Bankers Association, the Federal Reserve Board, Oct. 6, 2004, www.federalreserve.gov/boarddocs/speeches/2004/20041006/default .htm.

10. Myvesta.org, "Problem Debtors' Situations Worsening," press release, Oct. 9, 2003, http://myvesta.org/news/releases/100903PRClientSurvey.html.

11. *The Diagnostic and Statistical Manual of Mental Disorders* (DSM-IV), 4th ed. (Washington, DC: American Psychiatric Association, 1994), 176.

12. Ibid., 178.

13. Ibid., 176–79.

14. Ibid., 612.

15. Ibid., 650.

Chapter 3

1. Tian Dayton, *Trauma and Addiction: Ending the Cycle of Pain through Emotional Literacy* (Deerfield Beach, FL: Health Communications, 2000).

Chapter 4

1. Donna Boundy, "When Money Is the Drug," in *I Shop, Therefore I Am: Compulsive Buying and the Search for Self,* ed. April Lane Benson (Northvale, NJ: Jason Aronson Publishers, 2000), 5–12.

Chapter 7

1. Eric Halperin and Peter Smith, "Out of Balance," report by the Center for Responsible Lending, July 11, 2007, www.responsiblelending.org/issues/overdraft/ reports/page.jsp?itemID=33341925.

• • •

❖ About the Author ❖

Sally Palaian, Ph.D., is a clinical psychologist specializing in the treatment of addictive behaviors. Drawing from both her professional experience and her personal experience of growing up in a financially dysfunctional home, she developed many practical money-management techniques and tools. She has inspired countless individuals and couples to turn dreams into reality by making necessary lifestyle and financial decisions. She has served as an expert in the media on mental disorders and spending, most recently for MSN Money. *Spent* is her first book.

. . .